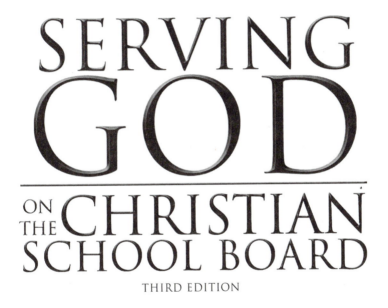

SERVING GOD

ON THE CHRISTIAN
SCHOOL BOARD

THIRD EDITION

SERVING
GOD

ON THE CHRISTIAN
SCHOOL BOARD

THIRD EDITION

Roy W. Lowrie, Jr.
and Roy L. Lowrie

Colorado Springs, Colorado

Purposeful Design Publications is the publishing division of the Association of Christian Schools International (ACSI) and is committed to the ministry of Christian school education, to enable Christian educators and schools worldwide to effectively prepare students for life. As the publisher of textbooks, trade books, and other educational resources within ACSI, Purposeful Design Publications strives to produce biblically sound materials that reflect Christian scholarship and stewardship and that address the identified needs of Christian schools around the world.

The views expressed in this publication are those of the author, and they may not necessarily represent the position of the Association of Christian Schools International.

Printed in the United States of America
16 15 14 13 12 11 10 09   4 5 6 7 8 9 10

Lowrie, Roy W., Jr., and Roy L. Lowrie
    Serving God on the Christian school board
    ISBN 978-1-58331-063-2 Catalog #6120

Cover Design: Kristopher Orr

Purposeful Design Publications
A Division of ACSI
PO Box 65130 • Colorado Springs, CO 80962-5130
Customer Service: 800-367-0798 • www.acsi.org

To my Peg, who sees me off to the board meeting and waits, and waits, and waits … and to the board members of Delaware County Christian School, Newtown Square, Pennsylvania—my friends and my coworkers in the Lord.

Behold, how good and how pleasant it is for brethren to dwell together in unity! (Psalm 133:1, KJV)

Contents

Foreword

It was the burden of the heart of Dr. Roy W. Lowrie, Jr., that Christian schools reflect in a pervasive and obvious way the name of the Savior that most of them bear. He understood what responsibilities the administrative and board leadership must carry out in order for that to be true.

If the Christian school board is to serve the school effectively, its members must have a clear understanding of what it means to be a part of an organization that works for the Kingdom by educating children. The dedicated volunteers who serve as school board members often come to that position with a strong commitment to the school but with little background in education and with limited knowledge of the functions of a policy-making body.

Biblical principles underlie the functioning of the Christian school board, and it is mainly by the Scriptures that its conduct must be judged. This work, first published in 1976, highlights the practical elements of school board service. Just as the school must be led and managed well to enjoy success in accomplishing its mission, the board must understand its policy-making functions and its role in support of the school's leadership. There is no more painful process in Christian schools than the conflict of a board and administrator that have not understood, agreed on, and accepted their appropriate roles. This book will be invaluable in helping school leaders to sort out their separate roles and to work together in biblical unity.

During his years of service to God at Delaware County Christian School, Dr. Lowrie learned, observed, and consulted with numerous other schools, assisting them in becoming institutions of integrity in their leadership structure. Out of his broad experience, Dr. Lowrie wrote this book as a means of helping Christian schools everywhere to become organizations of excellence.

Having served God in several Christian schools, Dr. Roy L. Lowrie took on the task of revising his father's work and preparing it for use by Christian schools today. The revision of *Serving God on the Christian School Board* is a strong contribution to Christian education today as well as an ongoing tribute to the memory of his father and his father's passion for Christian schools of excellence.

Derek Keenan
Vice President for Academic Affairs, ACSI

Preface to the First Edition

It is the purpose of this book to be of service to the school board of the local Christian school and to help the school's administrator as well. When the board and the administrator are serving God harmoniously, the ministry of the Christian school is a deep blessing to each.

It seems logical that part of the strategy of our adversary is to confuse the leadership of the school, but God is honored when things are done decently and in order. That includes the work of the board.

This book is not intended as a blueprint to be followed meticulously but as a guideline and a stimulus. Perhaps you will find several new ideas that can be used in your school. Perhaps stating things that your school board already does well will be an encouragement to continue in them.

Although educational administration is my major field, God has taught me a great deal through the board members of the Delaware County Christian School of Newtown Square, Pennsylvania. They were over me in the Lord for twenty-six years, and each left his mark upon me for good. For quite a few years I have also had the rich blessing of fellowship with board members and administrators throughout America. They too have taught me and ministered to me. School administration is, for me, a spiritual experience.

It is my desire that God will be pleased to minister to you through some of the thoughts that follow as you serve Him on your own Christian school board. My prayers and interest are with you.

Roy W. Lowrie, Jr.

Introduction

A special thank-you is extended to Dr. Roy L. Lowrie for his diligence in preserving the spiritual depth of his father's work, while making this revised edition applicable to twenty-first century Christian school leaders.

No one goes to school to learn how to serve on a school board. We simply learn on the job and assume that the certain way the board has always functioned must be proper board behavior. Unfortunately, the model we observe most is our local public school board. We have been led to believe that school boards make most of the operational decisions and give direction to the superintendent and principals through a voluminous board policy manual. Noted board consultant John Carver has said, Governance, as we have *inherited* it, is deeply flawed" (emphasis added).

Christian school trustees give generously of their time, talents, and expertise. They do an enormous amount of good for their schools. There is, however, one area of boardmanship that needs considerably more attention—that of fiduciary responsibility. Being a trustee for the owners, real or moral, is not fully understood in most cases. The capacity to participate in responsible trusteeship is not an innate ability. It must be learned consciously and developed intentionally. Few Christian school boards budget for the professional growth of their members. Many public school trustees are required to complete eight to twelve hours of training during their first year of service. Board governance is not management practiced at a higher level.

Serving God on a Christian school board is a holy calling, a ministry unto the Lord that deserves our best-informed effort. It behooves us to study board literature and to receive training so that we can carry out our responsibilities with knowledge and wisdom. We must serve in a way that honors our Lord.

While the criteria for serving on a Christian school board are quite similar to those of other private schools and nonprofit boards, the essential distinctive for Christian schools is that every trustee must be a mature Christian leader who is committed to thinking Christianly and modeling the teachings of Scripture in the boardroom, the school, and the community. Dr. Roy W. Lowrie, Jr., wrote, "Board members should be thinking Christianly when they come to the decisions that they have to make. Their decisions need to be as biblical as [their expectations of] the decisions of teachers and of administrators. This is why it is critical to have spiritually qualified board members.... It is better to have a smaller board of qualified people than to have a larger board with some being unqualified spiritually" (*Administration of the Christian School* [Colorado Springs, CO: ACSI, 1984], 305).

Roy began his journey in Christian education in 1952 when God led him to accept a teaching position at Delaware County Christian School (DCCS), a two-year-old school in suburban Philadelphia. In 1954, the board appointed him to the position of headmaster. Under Roy's leadership, DCCS soon became an exemplary Christian school that others sought to emulate during the era of the rebirth of the evangelical Christian school movement.

Few men have touched the hearts and minds of Christian school leaders as Dr. Roy W. Lowrie, Jr., has. He traveled the world, teaching about Christian education. His passion was that schools would be distinctively biblical in their leadership, philosophy, and methodology. Roy ministered humbly and effectively to thousands through speaking, writing, counseling, and mentoring. He was never too busy to receive a telephone call, listen to a problem, offer words of encouragement, and add another name to his prayer list. This ministry along with his twenty-eight years at Delaware County Christian School, his service as the executive director of the National Christian School Education Association, his tenure as president of the Association of Christian Schools International, and his constant study of God's Word gave him a profound understanding of the role of the board and the critical relationships between the board, board chair, and head of the school. Roy was one of the most respected Christian school leaders of the twentieth century, and he continues to be so today.

Serving God on the Christian School Board is a classic in Christian school literature. It is the single most significant book defining the quintessential characteristics and requirements for board service. It is a must-read for every school trustee and the first book that potential and new board members should be required to read. For veteran board members, this book will rekindle their passion for providing godly leadership. From the first chapter to the last, the reader will discover Roy's love for his Lord, his deep commitment to serve with excellence, and his passion for doing everything God's way. His constant reference throughout his life to "God's school system" makes abundantly clear his belief that Christ is the true head of every Christian school and that our duty is to discern His will in every aspect of the school. Christian schools are kingdom work.

1

INTRODUCTION TO CHRISTIAN SCHOOLS

Board members in a Christian school lead a spiritual institution.

The Christian school is a spiritual and educational endeavor in which the Spirit of God deals with the spirits of the students. The Christian school stands at the intersection of two things that God loves—children and truth. Christian school board members view their work from a spiritual perspective, through the Christian lens, because the things of the Spirit of God are spiritually discerned (1 Corinthians 2:14). The starting point to effective board service is a clear understanding of Christian education. Board members are philosophers as well as competent workers. Periodically, time should be invested in the board meeting for a discussion of foundational truths and new thoughts regarding the philosophy of Christian education. This practice has two purposes: it keeps the board sensitive to the reasons for which the school exists, and it edifies the board by helping members to grow in their understanding of Christian education.

The Christian school is not a nicer, safer, smaller, or more academic version of a public school. A Christian school is essentially different. It serves a different purpose than a secular school does, and its focus is different from that of a secular school. Christian education starts with the following beliefs: that God exists; that He has spoken through His Word, the Bible; and that He must not be ignored because He is the center of life. The secular school starts with the premise that God does not exist or that His existence is not relevant, that the Bible is merely the work of humans, that God ought to be ignored in the educational process, and that religion and faith are private issues that should not be a part of the content disciplines. With such different starting points, it is not surprising that the secular school and the Christian school are so dissimilar.

There are two primary purposes for Christian schools. Evangelistic schools are founded to convert the children of unbelieving families, whereas discipleship schools are established to help believing parents raise their children in the nurture and admonition of the Lord. The primary purpose of a school determines many of its policy, organizational, and curricular decisions. Each school develops and maintains a clear statement of purpose that serves as the guide to all other decisions. The mission statement is further explained in the school's philosophy. Whether the school's purpose is to convert nonbelievers or to disciple Christian children, the board should be careful to make decisions in keeping with that purpose. A discipleship school, for instance, should be careful to screen its applicants to be sure that the parents share the beliefs of the school.

Many schools attempt to fulfill both purposes, but doing so is challenging. Teachers largely determine the look and feel of Christian elementary schools, but the students more deeply influence the look and feel of Christian middle and high schools.

The Bible and Education

Educators wrestle with the question, Is there a vantage point from which a teacher or student can view truth and knowledge in proper perspective? Secular educators have concluded that no such vantage point exists, that each individual has a personal vantage point that is reality to that person. In short, truth is relative to the individual. Therefore, each person's truth ends at the tip of his or her nose.

There is a book, which is poorly understood in the educational world, that explains the true vantage point for all of life, including education. That book is the Bible, which our students can accept without question as the true vantage point on the authority of the Lord Jesus Christ. For He prayed, "Sanctify them by the truth; your word is truth" (John 17:17).

The Bible's teachings are absolute, dependable, and unchangeable. The psalmist wrote, "Your word, O Lord, is eternal; it stands firm in the heavens" (Psalm 119:89). Awesome judgments are pronounced against any person who adds or subtracts from the words of the Bible (Revelation 22:18–19). The Bible is absolute truth, and it is the foundation for education in the truth.

Origins

Thinking people, including philosophers, educators, and scientists, ponder the origins of the earth, the universe, and humankind. They realize that a person's view of origins determines his or her view of the purpose of humankind and the universe. But a successful search requires correct information. The Bible explains origins clearly. It reveals that God created the earth, the universe, and the first humans out of nothing by the authority of His spoken word, for His own glory. An education that denies the Creator's account of origins distorts all of life.

Purpose of Life

Education is designed to prepare students for life. But what is life all about? Educators may not avoid this question because the answer determines what educational goals they establish for their students. The Bible explains that God created humans for His pleasure. The purpose of life is to bring glory to God, the Creator-Redeemer (Revelation 4:11). This purpose is only accomplished when we receive Christ, are born again, and subsequently do the will of God.

To teach that life does not have purpose, or that the purpose cannot be known, or that the individual is at the center of life's purpose is to teach error. Instructors who do not know Christ and the Bible teach a false view of the purpose of life. They are "always learning but never able to acknowledge the truth" (2 Timothy 3:7). They are blind to the truth.

The Christian school prepares students not only for this life but also for the life hereafter. The Bible teaches that humans were created as eternal beings and that after this life we will spend an eternity either in heaven with God and His angels or in eternal hell. The Christian school prepares students for eternity.

Value System

Education instills in students an understanding of what is worthwhile, what is valuable, what is good. All teachers communicate a value system to their students through their instruction, and perhaps more, through their own lifestyles. There is no neutral teacher, no neutral school. Values are more effectively caught than taught. For this reason, Scripture warns about the deceptive influence of friends. Whether we realize it or not, whom we spend time with is who we become.

The best vantage point for building a value system is the Word of God, for it presents a redeemed value system. The issues of life are set in the right priority (Matthew 6:33), and the proper price tags are placed on things. American culture has placed an inflated value on material possessions, or "stuff." The problem with living for wealth is that we all have a God-shaped void in our souls, one that can be filled only through a personal relationship with the Lord Jesus Christ. The more we try to fill the eternal with the material, the emptier we become. We can stuff "stuff" into life, but it will never satisfy. The human soul finds rest in God alone.

Moral Standards

Many educators wish to instill in the hearts of their students a commitment to character, to doing what is right and living by moral standards. But moral standards must be built on a foundation of truth. Since the secular world has abandoned transcendent truth and has declared truth to be relative to every individual, secular morality has also become relative. Social mores have replaced biblical morals. Ethics are determined from polling data, not the Word of a higher authority. Instead of teaching students to appropriate eternal values into their lives, secular teachers encourage them to create and affirm their own personal standards.

The proof of moral relativism is in its fruit. American culture is reaping the fruit of improper instruction, and it is not a pretty sight. Secular educators may observe the horror of moral decay, but they are like someone in a hole with a shovel trying to dig himself out. The harder they try, the deeper in they get. Secular educators have no tool other than more and better-funded relativism to use in addressing the bankruptcy of character.

Only education from the moral vantage point of the Bible can produce good fruit. The Bible's moral standards are true because they were established and revealed by God. Not only are they pleasing to God, but also they are a benefit to the students. Today, students are under growing pressure to repudiate biblical morals and ethics. Right is being called *wrong*, and wrong is being called *right*. False moral teaching brings sorrowful results to children, young people, and adults; and the father of lies is reaping a harvest. Moral relativism and situational ethics are not God's vantage point for viewing morals.

Integration of Learning

Educators look for a unifying truth that will integrate all learning, binding it together as one intelligible whole. The Bible is that truth. "The fear of the Lord is the beginning of knowledge" (Proverbs 1:7). All the treasures of wisdom and knowledge are hidden in Christ (Colossians 2:3), and Christ is known through the Bible.

Teaching that depends on human reasoning as its integrating factor does not view truth from the right vantage point, for human reasoning always fractures and divides truth. The correct vantage point for the integration of learning is the Bible, the revelation from God. Truth is one because it has one Author.

In the Christian school, there are no secular subjects, for all truth is God's truth. Each course of study and the content of the whole curriculum revolve around the Lord Jesus Christ, God's Son, just as in the solar system the planets and comets revolve around the sun. The motion of the heavenly bodies makes sense only when a student understands gravity, motion, and the central role of the sun. The structure and application of learning makes sense only when a student understands and appreciates the centrality of the Son of God. The Christian school exists to proclaim the lordship of Christ in all areas of life. The unifying battle cry across the curriculum is "Jesus is Lord" (1 Corinthians 12:3).

There are many different philosophies of truth, but only the Bible teaches the right one (2 Timothy 3:16). The Bible is the key to the integration of life and learning.

Exclusion of the Bible
When the Bible is excluded from education, the sole vantage point of truth that integrates all learning is lost. The unifying truth is gone. The result is a distorted education that is not controlled by the Spirit of Truth but by the spirit of error, with educators who are "always learning but never able to acknowledge the truth" (2 Timothy 3:7). Like a ship adrift under a starless sky, they can measure the speed of their progress, but they can never arrive. Most secular educators do not know who they are because they do not know whose they are. They do not know where they are going because they do not know where they are, and they refuse to listen to the One who has charted their course.

The Bible and the Christian School
In the Christian school, the Bible is central, it is conspicuous, and it is authoritative. Christian educators know the Word of God, and they know who is at the center of their lives, their thinking, their subject matter, and their teaching. The Bible is not used just in Bible class but is openly integrated into all areas of the curriculum. This integration is not the artificial or mechanical infusion of Bible verses into an otherwise secular perspective on a curriculum area. Biblical integration is the natural process of the Christian mind that takes captive all the thoughts of humankind to make them obedient to the Lord Jesus Christ (2 Corinthians 10:5). Biblical integration is not primarily an issue about which textbooks to purchase. It is an issue about which teachers to hire. Secular teachers with Christian textbooks cannot do Christian instruction, whereas the mature Christian teacher can profess Jesus Christ as Lord of any textbook or literature. Christian textbooks are a helpful tool to assist teachers in integration, but for spiritual integration to be effective,

it must happen first in the teacher's mind. The curricular content is transformed by the renewal in the teacher's mind that restores the content to its proper position before God, the Creator-Redeemer (Romans 12:2).

The Bible is conspicuous in the Christian school because the Bible is at the center; it is frequently seen and heard on campus (Deuteronomy 6:9). It is present in the classroom, the cafeteria, the library, the computer lab, and the locker room. It is prominent in all the school's publications, in the school seal, on the bulletin boards, and on school T-shirts. The Word of God is conspicuous on the Christian school campus because it is central to the purpose of the school, and students learn that the Bible is central to life by seeing that it is conspicuous on campus. The prominence of Scripture challenges students to accept the claims of Christ.

The Bible is authoritative in all matters that it addresses (2 Timothy 3:16–17). God has revealed in Scripture all that is necessary for an abundant life. The problem with most Christians is that they do not know what the Bible contains and teaches. Because they do not know it, they cannot apply it, and they flounder through life, susceptible to every wind of teaching that blows through the church or community (Ephesians 4:14). The Christian school teaches the authority of the Bible by obedience to the claims of Christ. As students see teachers, administrators, and board members actively obeying Scripture, they learn to do the same. They begin to walk with the Lord in deeper knowledge and faith. If the Word of God is merely present in the school but not authoritatively applied in all areas of school life, the students will learn that Scripture is meant to be respected but not obeyed. May that never be!

Bible Classes in the Christian School
Bible class is not the sum of biblical instruction in the Christian school, but it is the most important part. Bible class contains the highest concentration of eternal truth and is the class that is taught with the most active opposition in the spiritual realm. Our adversary is not overly concerned about the Pythagorean theorem.

Only people who know the Word of God well and who know how to apply it to life should teach Bible classes. Not every Christian teacher, or even every Christian teacher in a Christian school, is able to teach the Word. The Bible class should have the best teachers and prominence in daily scheduling and in lesson planning. If a school is forced to choose, eternal truth is the most important value.

The content of the Bible class should be the Bible. With limited time available for teaching, the good may be the enemy of the best. Bible classes should not be group therapy sessions, current events seminars, or values clarification experiences. The student who goes through a Christian school should graduate with a systematic and working knowledge of the truths of God's Word as well as a clear understanding of God's claim on all of life. While this Christian mind is built to some extent in chapel, in science class, and on the basketball court, it is developed most formally in Bible class.

Prayer
"Do good to your servant, and I will live; I will obey your word. Open my eyes that I may see wonderful things in your law."
(Psalm 119:17–18)

For Discussion
1. Why is a Christian school a spiritual institution?

2. What are the foundational truths of the Christian philosophy of education?

3. What is your school's philosophy of education? Is it written anywhere? How is it communicated to your school family?

4. What is the role of the Bible in God's plan to reveal truth?

5. How do secular education and Christian education differ in their views of origins, the purpose of life, values, and moral standards?

6. What is meant by the integration of learning? How is biblical integration evident at your school?

7. What roles does the Bible play in the Christian school? In your school?

8. What principles for Bible class in a Christian school are offered in the chapter? Are these principles correct for your school? Are they being applied?

Going Deeper
1. Do you have any areas of your school that are not consistent with your Christian philosophy of education? What should be done about this inconsistency?

2. How has American culture been affected by the exclusion of the Bible and God from the educational system?

3. What evidence is there in your school that the Word of God is central, conspicuous, and authoritative? What changes could be made to give the Bible a more appropriate place in the school?

4. How is the Bible being taught in your school? Are all your teachers trained and capable in teaching the Bible? What are your students learning in Bible class? What evidence is there that Bible class is the most important area in your curriculum?

Other Activities

1. Have the board select one or two books that clearly present the Christian philosophy of education and adopt them as a reading/discussion assignment for all new board members.

2. Plan a series of home meetings for board members and their spouses to view and discuss ACSI's three videos on the Christian philosophy of education. The meetings will be most effective if they are scheduled on a night when there is no other board business.

2

THE PLACE OF THE BIBLE AND PRAYER IN THE BOARD

*The Bible is the center of all of life in a Christian school
because it is the Word of God, God's marching orders to His army.*

The Christian school exists to proclaim the lordship of Christ in all areas of life and to challenge students with God's claim to their hearts and lives.

If the Bible is to be central to the life of the school, it will be central to the life of the board. It will be considered in all decisions, made conspicuous in all meetings, and recognized as authoritative in every area it addresses. Christian school board members are people of the Book. They hold to Scripture as their final rule of faith and practice. They carry their policy manuals with the Bible on top.

The Bible in Board Meetings

Each meeting of the board, whether regular or special, should begin with a reading of appropriate Scripture followed by prayer. Fellowship among board members is nurtured when each board member takes a turn in leading devotions instead of the same one or two members leading every time. Leading is a growth experience for the members as they seek the Lord for the devotional. It helps other board members know the devotional leaders better as they share their thoughts from the Word.

The devotional period should not be rushed, for it is difficult to quiet the heart to hear Scripture when everyone is in a hurry. The time in the Word sets the tone for the meeting, allowing board members to get in tune with God's thoughts. The devotions are not a prelude to the meeting; they are a foundation on which the meeting is built. They are a priority. Boards should not tolerate a member who regularly joins the meeting after devotions.

Throughout the meeting, members must think and act from a biblical viewpoint. Board members who work in secular jobs may have to change some of their thinking and approaches to problems as they do the work of the board. This shifting of gears is essential, or the school will be run like any secular business. To illustrate, board members can apply Christian ethics in their secular jobs, but they cannot encourage their bosses to trust God and move a company ahead by faith. When board members come to the ministry of the school, they must view everything, not just ethics, from a biblical orientation.

Christian ethics should be practiced throughout the meeting. Much of the board's work is related to people, both in and out of the school. The Bible speaks clearly of the way Christians are to live with each other, and its principles must be applied. Board members need to encourage one another to do God's work in God's way. They should regularly ask the question that brought honor to the Bereans in Acts 17:11: What do the Scriptures say? There is often wisdom in tabling a motion until scriptural teaching on the topic can be reviewed and its principles brought to bear on the decision. While boards lead by their policies, they should live by their Bibles.

The Bible in a Board Member's Life

Personal holiness before the Lord is the primary prerequisite for serving God on the Christian school board. When the board members each make the Bible the lamp to their feet and the light to their path (Psalm 119:105), they naturally apply it to the work of the school when they get to the meeting, for they bring to the meeting that level of personal holiness before the Lord that characterizes each of them day by day.

The name of the Lord has been greatly shamed in some Christian schools by the sins of some board members. They were elected, but they were not holy, or they fell into sin following their election but were not honorable enough to resign from the board. Some schools carry deep wounds because of this dishonor, wounds that will take years to heal. Some will never heal. God forgives the sin of a repentant board member, but the consequences are not obliterated. What a board member sows, the school reaps; and as a leader, the board member will incur a stricter judgment.

Prayer in Board Meetings

The devotional period at the outset of the meeting should include time for earnest prayer. This prayer should be unhurried, allowing time for all to participate. If the prayer is conversational, members can feel free to pray more than once and can cover much in a short time.

The prayer time should include thanks to God for what He is doing in the school. When the going is tough, it is natural to petition God.

In spite of severe stress in the school, there is always reason to praise God. This is the sacrifice of praise, the fruit of our lips giving thanks to Him. Singing a hymn or spiritual song together at the end of devotions is a way to praise God together.

Prayer includes petitions for people and situations. God says that the fervent prayer of a righteous man accomplishes much (James 5:16). Board members must exercise care in talking about these petitions outside the meeting, for some should be held in strict confidence. There must be freedom in the meeting to pray about the real issues and problems.

As the board meeting progresses, individual members should lift their hearts quietly to God as the Spirit leads. This is a request for God to give wisdom, a desire to see Him work in the matter being discussed. This unobtrusive act does not disturb the flow of the meeting, for others need not know it. Such prayers need not be long. The Bible records some very short prayers (Nehemiah 2:4–5).

There are times when a knotty problem or an impasse occurs during the meeting. At such a time, it is extremely helpful for the chair to quietly stop the discussion as the board seeks the Lord about the matter. The chair may ask a particular person to pray, or she or he may open the door for prayer as the Lord leads. This prayer time often leads to new thinking and a solution to a matter. Another result may be a change in viewpoint and attitude on the part of some board members, allowing the impasse to be overcome. As a procedural matter, any board member should be able to call for a recess for prayer, and if one other member joins in the request, other board business should be tabled while the board prays. Prayerless business is godless business.

There is also wisdom in stopping for special prayer when the board is ready to vote on a decision that will make a significant impact on the school. Time spent waiting before the Lord for knowledge of His will in such matters is time well spent. The decision should be unanimous, or nearly so, for if the board is not united in its understanding of God's will in a matter, the confusion in leadership will have a negative effect on the school. The board should rarely move ahead on big issues when there is a close vote.

Prayer

"Lord, help our board members to be doers of the Word during the meeting and always. May they be holy people who know how and when to pray, and how to discern your will in board matters."

For Discussion

1. What is the appropriate use of the Bible for a Christian school board?

2. How should you conduct your devotional time at board meetings?

3. How is prayer currently a part of your board and committee meetings? What changes could be made that would make prayer a more vital part of your ministry?

4. Do you appropriately praise God for His provision and the protection of His school?

5. What resources are available on campus to help your board members and teachers grow in their ability to apply biblical principles to their responsibilities?

Going Deeper

1. Have you ever suspended discussion of a motion or a decision for the purpose of further research into biblical principles that apply? Why or why not? Should you make procedural changes to give biblical principles more prominence in your decision making?

2. Does your board view its policy-making role as rightly applying the authoritative Word of God to the current issue? Or does the board make decisions driven by the market, influential people, or expediency? What changes would help you apply the Bible actively and accurately in every decision?

3. Do your board policy manual, your employee manual, and your parent-student handbook include biblical references where appropriate? If not, why not, and what does their absence say to your families and students?

Other Activities

1. Review the central policies of the school and build a biblically based defense for each one.

2. The issue of finance is one that the Bible addresses frequently. Charge the finance committee with reviewing what the Bible has to say about giving, receiving, investing, lending, stewardship, and management of resources. Have them develop biblically based policies on fund-raising and financial management. Most schools will change some practices after doing this study.

3

MAJOR RESPONSIBILITIES OF THE BOARD

Selecting the right board members must be coupled with a good understanding of the responsibilities of the board.

Failure to comprehend the board's responsibilities will result in confusion, awkward situations, poor decisions, and oversights. Schools function well when the board clearly understands what board work is and judiciously avoids getting into work that belongs to the administrator. Boards are the corporate leadership of the school, and they provide a spiritual covering of the school. They establish the clear and broad policies of the school, hire the administrator, and evaluate her or his progress. They are the top legal and fiduciary authorities in the school. The administrator runs the school without violating the policy guidelines established by the board. She or he develops administrative policies and procedures to accomplish the goals of the school.

The board should clearly define in writing its own major responsibilities and those of any standing committees, and revise this organizational plan periodically as warranted. Certain committee responsibilities can be targeted to particular monthly meetings in which the designated committee will bring its recommendations. For instance, the finance committee may be charged with recommending the next year's budget each year at the December or January meeting. The board chair should regularly study the descriptions of board responsibilities to keep his or her leadership in step with the responsibilities described. The entire board should review each description periodically to keep their work in focus. As a significant part of their orientation to serving God on the board, newly elected members should learn what their responsibilities will be.

Exercise Spiritual Leadership

The school is a spiritual and educational enterprise, not a business venture. As the board charts the course for the school, it must seek, and find, knowledge of the Lord's will at every point. Such knowledge requires an understanding of biblical principles, the ability to pray about a matter to reach the proper decision, and the faith to believe God for all things. It also requires courage, for the school has adversaries of which Satan is one.

A secular, mechanical approach to problems falls short of the spiritual leadership demanded for a successful, effective school.

Spiritual leadership also includes being sensitive to the spiritual condition of the employees and students. Is there a spiritual fervor on campus? Is the Spirit of God accomplishing His work in the hearts and lives of the students? Spiritual maturation is difficult to measure, sometimes even to observe; but the board should be sensitive enough to spiritual matters to know whether its students are growing in Christ.

Boards should exercise spiritual leadership when they pray for the school's people and needs. A good portion of the time a Christian school board spends together should be invested in prayer. Some schools schedule more board prayer meetings than business meetings. Perfunctory prayer at the beginning or end of a board meeting is an indication that a board is operating in the flesh.

Establish Broad Policies

The board is responsible for establishing the major policies by which the school is governed. Sometimes these policies are developed as the school faces major problems, since policies are one means of addressing major or recurring problems. Boards should make a clear distinction between these broad policies and the operational and procedural policies that are set by the administration. Wise administrators and boards "borrow experience" by reading other schools' policy manuals and recommended policy manuals that are commercially available. While a school needs to work through each policy for itself, other schools' policy manuals may alert a board to a potential issue that it needs to address before a crisis occurs. The policy manual is invaluable to a new administrator or board member. The board chair, the board secretary, and the school's chief administrator are experts on the contents of the manual.

The traditional approach to school policies is to have the board discuss and approve policies for the vast majority of recurring issues that an administrator faces. Standing committees are often formed around the major administrative areas of responsibility, and the committees discuss and recommend policy revisions to the board. The weakness of this approach has been that boards often focus too much attention on making policies in minute areas and ignore doing the work that only boards can do.

A more current approach to board policy is advocated by John Carver in his Policy Governance ® model. The Carver model more clearly differentiates board responsibilities and administrative duties. Policy Governance is a very formal way of structuring boards that is intended to avoid the ineffectiveness and confusion inherent to so many organizations. In thumbnail fashion, Carver boards establish policies in only four areas: Ends Policies, Governance Process Policies, Governance-Staff Linkage Policies, and Executive Limitation Policies. A thorough overview of the Carver model is available from many sources, such as *Boards That Make a Difference* and *Empowering Boards for Leadership* by John Carver.

Plan Strategy

A good board spends much of its time looking ahead and establishing institutional goals. It should plan where it wants the school to go and then challenge the administrators to strategize on how to get the school there. Over the years, the quality of the board's strategic planning becomes evident. Boards do not plan to fail, but some fail to plan. Planning touches every area of development, such as the master site plan and the projection of enrollment, facilities, needed faculty, and finances. While much of this work is done initially by the administration, the plan is reviewed, honed, and adopted by the board. Some of the growth steps in the life of the school are too big to implement in one year. These steps will seldom be taken if the school is locked into a "next year only" planning cycle.

Many helpful resources enable boards to effectively define the future of their institutions as the Lord wills. One beneficial approach is to brainstorm and then prioritize the strengths, weaknesses, opportunities, and threats (SWOT) of the school. Strengths and weaknesses are internal to the school. Opportunities occur externally in the wider community or society, and threats are internal or external. SWOT analysis helps focus attention on enhancing strengths, addressing weaknesses, seizing opportunities, and protecting against threats.

Hire a Competent Administrator

There is a common saying in Christian school administration that the most important job of the board is to recruit, hire, and retain a competent administrator. The administrator is the chief school officer. His or her work has the greatest single influence on the school.

The second biggest job of the board is to empower the administrator to run the school. The board is not to be involved in the day-to-day management of the school. The administrator and board should work in harmony, but each must understand the other's responsibilities, and they must not interfere with each other. The board establishes policies, and the administrator leads the school within the boundaries defined by those policies.

Quality schools are built by administrators who received training and experience as teachers and who then go on to earn at least a master's degree in school leadership, preferably in Christian school administration. Teachers respect and follow these administrators, knowing that they understand what it is like to be a teacher. Administrators who have not trained as school administrators are unprepared for educational leadership even though they love God. They should be professionally prepared for school administration just as a Christian physician is prepared to practice medicine. There are no shortcuts.

An administrator who has not earned a graduate degree cannot exhort teachers to earn one. In schools, there is a strong relationship between the preparation of the administrator and that of the teachers. Strong teachers prefer to serve under well-qualified administrators whose knowledge, ability, and training they can respect.

Work with the Administrator
The board-administrator relationship is the key relationship in the school. The administrator's attitude toward the board is important to her or his morale. Strong administrators do not make long-term commitments under weak or dictatorial boards. The board does not keep secrets from the administrator and does not meet without the administrator present, except for the regular evaluation of the administrator and determination of the administrator's compensation. Secrecy breeds division and distrust. It destroys the school.

Evaluate the Administrator
The chief administrator is the only employee directly evaluated by the board. Part of the growth process for the administrator is an annual evaluation of his or her performance. The evaluation should be done by the entire board in executive session. It should be the first item on the agenda of the meeting in December, or January at the latest. It is not fair to the administrator to conduct such an evaluation at the end of a typical board meeting.

The basis for the evaluation is the administrator's job description and institutional goals. The board should work through the evaluative criteria point by point and reach a consensus on each item. If the board did not use the items in the job description as the evaluative criteria, the board members would individually evaluate according to their own ideas of what the administrator should do rather than the responsibilities defined in the job description. The board chair should report the annual evaluation to the administrator in private the day after the evaluation meeting. It is likely to be intimidating to an administrator for the entire board, or even the executive committee, to present him or her with the results.

The evaluation should be positive. Strengths should be noted, for even strengths need encouragement and improvement. Weaknesses should be well defined, with suggestions for improvement. The board should specifically identify areas of weakness and describe what satisfactory performance would look like in the area of responsibility. The board should provide the time and support needed for the administrator to strengthen areas of weakness. When the board chair concludes the report, he or she should ask the administrator for an evaluation of the board's performance, again with clear suggestions for improvement.

Dismiss the Administrator

There are times when it is necessary to dismiss an administrator. Such a decision should never be taken lightly or without much prayer over a suitable period of time. The board not only holds the livelihood of the administrator but should also be concerned about the spiritual well-being of the administrator's family.

Administrators should be dismissed for moral failure. The school is not strengthened by retaining a leader who has been disqualified for ministry, regardless of the political or professional skills the leader possesses. Leaders are not perfect people, but they must live above reproach in the community to be qualified to serve.

Most administrators are removed from their positions for reasons other than moral turpitude. This decision should only be made at a duly called meeting in conjunction with a full evaluation of the performance of the administrator. Dismissal should be the last step in a process focused on helping the administrator to improve in areas of deficiency. Boards should specifically identify areas of weakness and describe what satisfactory performance would look like in the area of responsibility. If improvement is not satisfactory over a reasonable time, the administrator should be dismissed or notified that she or he will not receive a contract for the following year. It is generally in the best interest of the school community for the administrator to complete the current school year.

Administrators should be told by January at the latest if their contract will not be renewed. A board may choose to either buy out the rest of the administrator's contract or have her or him complete the year. If a board chooses to release an administrator during the school year, the administrator deserves a fair severance package. One rule of thumb is that an administrator should receive salary and benefits for a period equal to six months plus one month for each year of service at the school.

Follow Government Regulations

The Bible teaches Christians to obey the government unless the government clearly requires what God forbids or forbids what God requires. In the United States, education is the responsibility of each state and not of the federal government. States vary markedly in their requirements for private schools and in the degree to which they enforce their requirements.

Biblically, of course, education is a parental responsibility. All states and many local governments establish their own requirements for their public and private schools. Boards ensure that schools are operating honestly and in compliance with legal requirements.

Reports to government agencies must be handled according to the agencies' requirements and within their time limits. Particular care must be taken with social security, federal income tax, and IRS codes. Applications for legal charters, tax exemption, and eligibility for foundation grants are best prepared with professional counsel. The attorney's and accountant's fees are usually a wise investment.

Exercise Financial Responsibility

Legally and ethically, a school board has a fiduciary responsibility. It is ultimately responsible for the finances of the school, both to the government and to God as a steward of His resources. The school's financial position has a significant influence on its effectiveness in the hearts and lives of students. While Christian schools are not started for financial gain, they cannot fulfill their spiritual and academic missions without sound financial planning and management. Quality boards fulfill their fiscal responsibilities and achieve financial stability while developing quality.

The board usually receives a current and understandable report about the present financial position and a report of recent financial activity of the school at each meeting. If a board has a finance committee, the administration and the committee should scrutinize these reports before the board meeting. A board is not able to fulfill its legal responsibility in the area of finance if it does not understand the financial reports it receives. In addition to the regular reporting that is prepared by the administration, or perhaps the board treasurer, the school board will personally review the annual audit report. Every school should have an annual, external audit.

Achieving and maintaining fiscal responsibility depends on the following administrative tasks: (1) complete trust in God for the money needed to develop the school, (2) careful construction of the annual budget,

(3) control of expenditures to prevent overspending the budget, (4) sufficient tuition to balance the budget, (5) clear policies for handling delinquent tuition accounts, (6) a realistic view of the amount of money to be received through gifts, (7) promotion for the receipt of gift money, (8) annual external audits, (9) annual financial reports to donors and members, (10) extreme care in projecting and controlling the costs of new construction, (11) realism in projecting the actual operational costs of a new building, (12) and accurate projections of future enrollment and finances.

Each of the tasks listed above is an administrative responsibility first. Boards, however, must provide the necessary monitoring to be confident that these tasks are being accomplished well.

Encourage Quality People and Programs

Although buildings and facilities are needed, teachers and staff members are the gold in the bank. Good boards encourage the administrator to seek and hire the best possible teachers. Board policies should enable the administrator to employ God's best for the school.

A sure sign of serious problems in a school is rapid turnover among teachers and staff members. Quality is never achieved in schools where the faculty lounge has a revolving door.

Each year the board should ask the administrator for recommendations for the improvement of the salary schedule and benefits, such as a major medical plan, and should be sure that the budget the administrator proposed incorporates these changes. It is important in the early years of the school to get moving on offering better salaries and benefits. Sometimes schools move slowly in this area, and they put unfair financial burdens on the faculty and staff. Financial decisions should not always favor parents over teachers. To put it another way, tuition should be high enough that the school can pay its teachers adequately, trusting God to supply parents with enough money. A rule of thumb for adequate compensation in most settings is whether a teacher can reasonably expect to raise a family.

The administrator is responsible for the professional evaluation of the staff and needs to be empowered to make decisions about which faculty members are offered contracts for the next year. However, dismissal of an employee during a contract is a potentially litigious and difficult issue. The board can protect the school from potential liabilities by retaining the authority to dismiss, as recommended by the administrator, an employee who is under contract.

Provide Adequate Buildings and Equipment

Christian teachers are hard workers, for they do not view teaching as just a job but as a calling. However, having conscientious teachers does not cancel the need for proper facilities and equipment. Good teachers are even better when they have good tools.

It usually takes time for a school to get property, construct buildings and athletic fields, and equip and supply the classrooms. The board prayerfully establishes policies that enable the administrator to improve these resources without undue tension or financial disaster. When facilities and equipment are inadequate, the students and the teachers pay the price. There are no shortcuts, even in the Christian school, to quality education. Buildings need not be luxurious, but they should be large enough and designed well enough to support a high-quality program.

Some existing church buildings can be used as a school, but many are not adequate for school use. Most Sunday school rooms do not have the 800 to 1,200 square feet needed for a school classroom, not to mention the space needed for such rooms as the library and computer lab. Very early in the process of a church considering starting a school, it is wise to have a professional evaluation of a building's adequacy for use as a school. Experience indicates that it is better to design a church-school educational building as a school and use it as a Sunday school than to build small classrooms that are typical in a Sunday school building and try to use a church as a school.

Encourage Good Public Relations

Good schools have an active program of public relations. While the administrative team is responsible to do the activity of public relations, the board should write policies that encourage good public relations and evaluate the administrator in this area.

The school's publics—groups to which the school must continually be represented—include the following: (1) parents of the students, (2) local churches, (3) local communities, (4) alumni, (5) parents of alumni, and (6) donors and friends of the school. The presentation of the school must always be honest. Press releases and pictures should be of top quality. Enough money must be budgeted to do effective advertising and produce attractive literature. It is a mistake to cut corners in public relations.

Satisfied parents and students are a school's best public relations agents. Appealing literature and an adequate budget do not compensate for dissatisfaction within the school family. A school that is doing the job will attract new students.

Board members are key persons in public relations, for each is a special representative of the school. Their Christian testimony before believers and unbelievers influences the way outsiders think about the school. Board members, through their attitude and behavior within the school family, influence the way those involved with the school think about it. Disgruntled board members harm the school and should resign or be replaced.

Exercise Final Authority

The school's chief administrator works under the board. It is a serious error for a school administrator not to respect the board or to fail in following its policies. Similarly, it is a serious mistake for a board to meddle in administration or abdicate its responsibility as the final authority.

The board's authority is not to be exercised in a high-handed manner. There are times in the history of a Christian school, however, when strong, firm action is needed. The board will recognize such times when they occur and will make the correct decisions according to biblical principles without respect of persons. Personnel or family issues should always go through the administrator. If the board draws back from tough decisions, the school will pay the consequences later, often for years to come. Sometimes the proper exercise of authority seems to create new problems, but those problems are preferable to the problems that go unresolved because the board is afraid.

Prayer

"Dear God, help the board fulfill its responsibilities by giving the members a clear understanding of the Scripture that is applicable to the matters to be faced. Give each member wisdom from above. Give each one courage to do what is right."

For Discussion

1. Why is it important to hire and empower a competent administrator?

2. Are any of the factors listed under fiscal stability not present in your school? If so, which ones?

3. What are the strengths and weaknesses of your school's buildings and grounds? What improvements or additions are needed?

4. With what public agencies and entities does your school interact? Who is responsible to maintain relationships with whom?

5. How important is accreditation to your school? Where are you in the process?

Going Deeper
1. How can your board increase its effectiveness in spiritual leadership?

2. If you were able to recruit and retain the ideal faculty for your school, what would be their distinguishing characteristics? What would they need to be effective at your school over the long haul?

Other Activities
1. Visit several schools with strong facilities. Walk through them with an administrator and gather ideas for future development at your school.

2. Encourage your administrator to offer several of your veteran teachers to serve on visitation committees for different accrediting agencies. The ideas they garner will more than pay for the substitutes you hire during their absence.

3. Form an ad hoc committee to research the Carver model of board governance and report their findings and recommendations to the board. Include in the research the experiences of other Christian schools that have moved to the Carver model.

4

ORGANIZATIONAL STRUCTURE OF THE BOARD

God is a God of order.

God accomplishes His plans through human authority. There is a divine chain of command within the Trinity itself in which the Son is submissive to the Father and the Spirit is submissive to the Son. It seems reasonable to conclude that God's work should also be done in an orderly manner. Christian schools require a structure of authority, from which is derived the chain of command.

The organizational structure of a new school should be defined carefully and in writing, and it should be adhered to in all issues in succeeding years. The structure can be revised if necessary, but the school must be careful to observe any requirements for making such revisions to parts of the corporation constitution or bylaws.

Organizational Patterns

Christian schools are organized along three major patterns. Category I schools are church sponsored. The school is an integral ministry of the local church, and the church exercises direct authority over the school. Category II schools are church related. They are separately incorporated and operated as an auxiliary ministry of a church. Category III schools are independent of a local church. They are either a parent-sponsored school; a board-sponsored school, operated by a self-perpetuating school board; or a proprietary school, controlled by an individual or entity. Within these broad categories, many structural nuances differentiate individual schools.

Each of the organizational patterns has strengths and potential weaknesses. A church-sponsored or church-related school is usually an efficient use of facilities, keeping tuition lower and providing clear spiritual oversight. However, mixing church politics with school politics causes difficulties for both ministries when problems occur in either. In parent-sponsored schools, the board is very attentive to the needs of families because the members' own children are usually enrolled there, but these schools can be slow to raise tuition as needed because the parents vote on budget issues. Independent board schools have the advantage of being able to be decisive and the disadvantage of being open to control by a very few individuals.

The trend in recent years has clearly been toward independent boards. Independent boards are more prevalent among larger schools. Some schools start as church related or sponsored, but as they grow, the needs of the school increase to the point that they distract from the church. Often these schools are then transferred to the authority of an independent board. This migration is often healthy for the school and the church.

Models of Boardmanship

Most school board committee structures have standing committees. For instance, there are education, facilities, and personnel committees. Every important part of the school is reflected in a board committee, ensuring many checks and balances on decision making. Sometimes this committee structure results in boards meddling in administrative responsibilities or an administrator not being fully empowered to do his or her job. Often committee members who want to help cause more harm than good because they do not know where their responsibilities stop and where the administrator's begin.

In the early years, a school often requires the combined efforts of many volunteers to get going. However, at some point, the school hires a competent administrator, and the responsibilities of the board change. If committees with titles of administrative functions are used, their responsibilities must be clearly defined to avoid confusing board business with administrative business. Many boards choose to have only ad hoc committees.

Board Meeting Schedules

Many boards in smaller or younger schools meet monthly. There are sufficient issues and a limited administration, so the frequent meetings are a benefit to the school. A mature school with an experienced administrative team may have fewer board meetings in a year, often between four and six. Some schools add meetings for the sole purpose of prayer, often early in the morning.

It is wise to schedule meetings well in advance. Board members who live nearby will not have travel problems in attending meetings. However, some may have scheduling problems because of their work.

Committees of the Board

Committees that function properly can expedite the board's work and prevent a serious problem in efficiency. The committees do the legwork and bring their best thinking before the board for action. The board need not accept all the recommendations of its committees automatically or without revision. In turn, the board must respect the work of the committees and consider their recommendations carefully, or the committee members will become discouraged, feeling that the board does not listen to their recommendations. Procedurally, a committee recommendation may come to the floor of a board meeting as a seconded motion. That means that the board need not seek a second and must respond to the recommendation in some manner.

A standing committee, one that is always in existence, focuses on a particular area of need or expertise and makes recommendations as those issues come before the board. An ad hoc committee is established for a particular purpose, and when the task is completed, the committee reports to the board and then ceases to exist. A finance committee is usually a standing committee, whereas a site location committee would be an ad hoc committee. Schools vary significantly in their use of standing and ad hoc committees. Although standing committees have the benefit of expertise in a needed area, they also have the unfortunate tendency to creep over from policy into administration. Ad hoc committees have the advantage of getting their work done efficiently. The clear trend in recent years is for boards to function with few standing committees, if any, encouraging boards to do board work and minimizing the problem of boards getting involved in administration.

The chairs of every board committee, and usually the majority of the members, are board members. Board committees may also include other people approved by the board who are willing to serve in their area of expertise or experience. The agenda for the regular meetings of the board includes an opportunity and expectation for each committee chair to report to the full board. The length and importance of each report will vary according to the present status of the school. Any recommendations made to the board should be communicated along with the agenda to each member prior to the meeting to allow time for reflection and consideration.

The administrator and board chair serve as ex officio members of each committee. They are usually nonvoting members but are invited to every meeting and attend most of them.

The board chair is responsible for appointing the committee chairs and may serve on a committee but should not have the additional responsibility of chairing any other than the executive committee, which consists of all the board officers. The committee chair serves for one year. The next year's board chair, who may be new, has the prerogative of changing committee chairs as he or she thinks appropriate. There is value in having the chairs of some committees serve more than one year, but it is not wise to allow a chair to become entrenched. Some degree of change each year is healthy, for each chair brings strengths and weaknesses to a committee.

Executive Committee

The officers of the board form the executive committee. They are often empowered by the board to take action on behalf of the board on emergency issues that may arise between board meetings. They also handle issues that are extremely sensitive, in a manner that is highly confidential. It is not necessary for every board member to know everything about the school. Only the executive committee, however, should handle the extremely confidential matters. Not many matters will warrant such treatment.

The board as a whole handles most of its business rather than turning much of it over to the executive committee. When the executive committee handles too much business, it becomes too powerful, and the wholesome checks and balances that are in play when the whole board meets are reduced.

Organizational Charts

One of the early documents an administrator should develop and maintain is the organizational chart, which expresses graphically the school's chain of command. The chart is an important part of the board manual, the employee manual, and the parent-student manual. It is the answer to many questions and prevents a few problems. Everyone in the school community should have a working knowledge of the authority structure in the school. Everyone should also know how problems are to be solved by applying the Matthew 18 principle: First, deal with matters as far down in the chain of command as possible and then move up step-by-step if necessary.

Within many Christian schools, there is also an informal power structure, known as a "wild center," which is not represented on the official organizational chart. A wild center could be a secretary who is married to a board member or simply two teachers and three board members or their wives who meet weekly for coffee. A wild center is any vortex of power or influence that short-circuits or circumvents the formal authority structure. Information, opinion, and even decisions bypass certain levels in the chain of command. While personal relationships can be wonderful and helpful, board members and staff members in a Christian school need to be careful to separate their personal and professional contacts. The professional responsibilities of managing God's school should always be accomplished through the formal power structure He establishes. For a biblical illustration of the damage that a wild center can do, read the history of the exodus of God's people, especially what happened when God's leader went up the mountain to receive the law.

Prayer

"Lord, help us discern the best organizational structure for our school, and help us to minister within that structure according to biblical principles. Thank you for the ministry of the Spirit among us in showing us how to function harmoniously."

For Discussion

1. Why is it important to know the organizational structure of your school?

2. Is the formal exercise of authority really a means God uses to accomplish His work in your school?

3. Which of the major organizational patterns best describes your school's design?

4. What are the benefits of standing committees and ad hoc committees?

5. What are the duties of each officer on your board? How are the officers selected? What are their terms of office?

Going Deeper

1. Are the responsibilities of the board and each board committee clearly written and understood by the board members, or is this an area that needs work? What modifications to your plan should you consider?

2. What wild centers exist in your school? What are the potential benefits and dangers in them? Should the board act to address the dangers?

3. Is your current schedule of board meetings conducive to fulfilling your board's purpose, or does it encourage you to cross over into administrative issues?

5

SELECTING BOARD MEMBERS

If a Christian school is to achieve and maintain high quality,
the school board needs good members.

The selection of board members is important when the school begins, and it continues to be important in succeeding years. The quality of the school is a direct product of the quality of its board and the administrators it chooses to lead the school. Because of the significance of choosing board members, this discussion will consider the direct influence of the board on the school, the board as part of the school's reputation, biblical qualifications for board members, and the balance that is needed on the board. Sections will also address the nominating committee, procedures for nominations, election procedures, and appointed and self-perpetuating boards.

Influence of the Board

The work of the board touches everyone involved in the school. Board members usually work behind the scenes, but their policies and decisions govern the school. Board influence comes from several directions. The primary function of the board is to set sound policies, which act as boundaries and guidelines within which the administrator directs the school.

Wise board members establish sound policies. Characteristics of wise board members include the following: (1) knowing Christ Jesus as Lord, for in Him are hidden the treasures of wisdom and knowledge; (2) knowing the Scriptures, for they reveal the wisdom of God; (3) actively seeking wisdom from above, as a result of praying in faith; and (4) applying scriptural principles to Christian school matters when determining policies. It is possible to be a board member and not be a wise one.

Spiritual Qualifications for Board Members

The Bible does not mention the Christian school board, but it does lay down qualifications for leadership in 1 Timothy 3 and Titus 2. These spiritual qualifications may reasonably be applied to the leaders of any Christian organization that purposes to operate biblically. The Bible lists the following requirements for born-again leaders: blameless, temperate, sober-minded, of good behavior, gentle, hospitable, able to teach, discreet, chaste, not given to wine, not violent, not greedy for money, not quarrelsome, not covetous, not a novice, and not double-tongued. Leaders must also be teachers of good things and have a good testimony among those who are outside. They must lead their own house well and have their children in submission. Their spouses must not be slanderers but rather be reverent and faithful in all things.

A Christian school that does not adopt and maintain biblical requirements for board membership cannot function in a thoroughly biblical manner. Spiritually unqualified leaders may not expect to experience the full blessing of God. Just one unqualified member can significantly damage a Christian school board.

It is possible that a board member who was spiritually qualified when coming on the board will experience a personal change, or a change to a family member, that disqualifies him or her for membership on the board. When that sad event occurs, the board member should resign, and the resignation should be accepted. If the board member does not resign, the board must make the difficult choice of removing that person from the board. Removal takes courage, but it is right. Every school should have a simple mechanism, such as a two-thirds vote of the board, to remove a member from office. When the time comes to use such a procedure, the issue will be so difficult that the board will be thankful to have an uncomplicated procedure.

Whether elected or appointed, board members must believe that the school is of God and have it in their hearts to serve Him well in their position. Upon joining the board, members should publicly agree with the school's statements of faith and purpose. The board secretary may receive annually from all board members a written reaffirmation of both statements. Members who share the vision of the school but are appointed automatically because of the church office they hold, or board members who accept because nobody else will do it, are not helpful. A smaller board made up of people whose hearts have been touched by God on behalf of the school is better than a larger board that has some indolent or unqualified members.

No board member should be selected because of financial position or giving. Such favoritism, while it may be advantageous financially, is clearly sin and grieves the Holy Spirit (James 2:4). The gifts of giving and of ruling are separate spiritual gifts (Romans 12:8). Board membership is a spiritual office in a spiritual institution, and it should not be awarded to the highest bidder.

The initial board of a new school is formed with great caution to be certain that high standards are established from the outset. For example, it is unwise to ask for volunteers to serve on the board. Some who volunteer may not be qualified, and an unqualified member can be a serious matter. The person may have strong influence for many years at the highest level of the school. It is prudent to start with a few select members and build up gradually with properly qualified people.

An effective mechanism to ensure that new board members will be qualified for spiritual service is to have the current board and administration review the spiritual qualifications of all potential candidates. If two or more current board members think someone is not qualified, that person should not become a board candidate. In some schools, a candidate would need unanimous support. Certainly, a candidate should not be selected on a close, split vote.

Pragmatic Considerations for Board Members

Variety and balance are wholesome qualities in a board. Boards seeking candidates may consider several pragmatic issues as long as these are clearly secondary to the spiritual qualifications. No potential board member who is marginal or disqualified for spiritual service should be placed on the board, even if there are many apparent benefits to having the person serve. Sometimes, practical gifts can be used on a committee of the board even when the person is not qualified to serve on the board itself. For example, a commercial realtor may be of great assistance on the site search committee even if he or she is not qualified to give spiritual leadership.

Church Representation

It is healthy to have members from several churches, especially if the school is not operated by a single church. Care must be taken to keep any one church from exercising too much influence. Board members do not represent the interests of a church, but rather the interests of the school, unless the school was founded as a cooperative ministry of two or more churches.

Children of Board Members

Board members must be committed to the philosophy of Christian education. This commitment should carry over to the education of their own children. If a board member has school-age children, they should be enrolled in the Christian school. However, there are occasions in which the special needs of their child cannot be served within the program of their Christian school.

Occupational Representation

The Bible says there is wisdom in many advisers (Proverbs 15:22). Since each board member acts from his or her own working background, it is helpful to have some different occupations represented. Regardless of occupation, though, all board members need to be educationally oriented in order to make decisions that are sound from the standpoint of education and ministry.

Independent Team Members

The board needs people who are independent thinkers, willing to speak up, willing to be in the minority. At the same time, all members must be willing to work harmoniously with the others. The board is a body, not a collection of members. It is a team, not a collection of prima donnas.

Veterans and New Members

To gain and maintain stability, the school needs a nucleus of board members who stick with it over a period of years. It takes faith in God and years of hard work to acquire property for the school, to build facilities, to add a high school, and to hire and keep top personnel. Boards made up of short-term members have trouble accomplishing these tasks. At the same time, it is healthy for the board to have a steady influx of new members, who bring fresh perspective and enthusiasm and help the board to keep functioning with vigor. Board members do not reach their prime effectiveness until they have served for three years. A board policy requiring members to rotate off the board every three years may provide a way to graciously out-process ineffective board members, but the policy keeps the board immature. A better policy is to have one-third of the board members stand for renomination and reelection each year. More schools are hurt by perpetual immaturity than are helped by the continual influx of new members.

Nominations and Elections

The procedures for nominations and elections are usually spelled out in the school's constitution and bylaws that are binding legal documents. Boards must take care to follow them consistently. The following ideas are one way to deal with nominations, but they should not be followed if they differ from the school's constitution. The key factors to remember in the selection of board members are that the board should maintain control of the nominating process and that prospective board members should be trained before they are ultimately selected or approved.

Nominating Committee

In many schools, the entire board serves as the nominating committee. The nominating committee is the key to developing a quality board.

If this committee has the will and courage to screen candidates properly, only qualified candidates will stand for election. When all candidates are properly qualified, the quality of the board will be preserved no matter which candidates are elected.

The composition of the nominating committee is usually specified in the bylaws. If it is not, appointing these committee members is one of the most important things the chair ever does. If the school has an open nominating process, it should adopt a strict training and screening process to ensure that the candidates who stand for office are spiritually qualified to serve.

Ranking the Nominees

The nominating committee is charged with bringing the strongest slate possible into the election. One way to do so is to rank the potential candidates in order of preference. These are logical steps to follow: (1) list all the potential nominees that the committee approves, (2) have each committee member or board member vote *qualified* or *not qualified* for each nominee and then list the nominees on a slip of paper in order of preference, (3) give these slips to the secretary of the nominating committee, and (4) let the secretary average the ratings and establish a master list showing the rankings in the thinking of the entire committee. A computerized spreadsheet makes the calculating and sorting almost instantaneous. If two or more current board members think a person is not biblically qualified for spiritual service, the board should seriously consider whether the candidate should stand for office.

The Number of Nominees

It is wise to have several more nominees than vacancies. If the nominating committee brings the same number of nominees as there are vacancies, the committee itself is actually doing the electing. If the committee brings just one more nominee than there are vacancies, it becomes a very personal defeat for the one not chosen.

Self-Perpetuating Boards

Many Christian schools are adopting the self-perpetuating board model in which the board is independent and selects its own members. When a board is self-perpetuating, heavy responsibility for finding a quality board is placed on fewer people, who must make their selections carefully, giving special weight to a candidate's conviction that it is God's will for him or her to serve on the board. This process is important, for the person invited to serve does not have to run for election.

Selection of Officers

Officers are prescribed in the constitution and bylaws. In most schools, officers are elected annually, and they consist of a chair, vice chair, secretary, and treasurer, with the duties and powers that are usually attached to the offices. A job description for each officer should be included in the board policy manual. This job description becomes the foundation for officer evaluation. The chair calls and runs meetings, sets the agendas, and appoints any committees. The vice chair serves in the role of the chair when the president is absent. The secretary is responsible for accurate minutes of the meetings and for correspondence. The treasurer ensures that the board has accurate and timely reports of the financial position and activity of the school.

Length of Board Term

The school's constitution and bylaws usually define the length of a term of service on the board. A board member's term should be neither too short nor too long. To illustrate the first problem, board members who must go off after only one term do not have enough time to get deeply into the ministry. In addition, the board officers are inexperienced since they hold their positions only for a short time. Conversely, if members stay on and on, the board is denied fresh blood. Such members may develop tendencies to get involved in the administration of the school, especially if they hold top board offices over many years. One approach is to require members to go off the board for at least a year after two or three successive terms, the average term being three or four years. It is also healthy to change board officers periodically so that no one person becomes entrenched in his or her position.

Size of the Board

The size of the board is usually specified by the constitution and bylaws and is related to how much work there is to do. Often, the larger the school, the more work there is and the larger the board should be. In general, boards run from seven to fifteen members. With fewer than seven members, it is hard to conduct business when several are absent. With more than fifteen, the board may become unwieldy and inefficient. Schools are well served when the board focuses on the quality of the board members above the quantity of board members.

Prayer

"Father, give our school your wisdom in nominating or appointing board members. Work in and through the entire selection process, and bring to office the persons of your own choice to serve you as Christian school board members."

For Discussion

1. Do the biblical qualifications for spiritual leadership apply to board membership at your school? What safeguards are in place to ensure that all nominees who stand for office are qualified?

2. What does the Bible teach about giving preferential treatment to the rich? Should a potential candidate's financial status be taken into consideration?

Going Deeper

1. Review the biblical criteria for spiritual service and write a list of evidence for each criterion that would indicate its presence or absence in a potential candidate for school board. In other words, what does a qualified person look like, and what does an unqualified person look like?

2. Describe the "balance" that currently exists on your school board. Are there any areas of excessive power or influence? Are there any areas of need or weakness?

3. What do you have in place to ensure a healthy mix of veterans and new blood on your board? Are your policies working? What is the average length of service on your board?

Other Activities

Do a policy audit of the bylaws and policies of the school board to see whether they address all the issues discussed in this chapter. What issues, if any, are not addressed?

6

THE BOARD-ADMINISTRATOR RELATIONSHIP

The key relationship in the Christian school is between the administrator and the board.

The relationship between the administrator and the board bears the heaviest brunt of satanic opposition against the school. It must be carefully nurtured, and it requires a continuous and spiritually mature application of biblical principles by each party. Strong schools are established only when the administrator and board work effectively together over a number of years.

Confidence in leadership is essential in a voluntary organization. For a school to be managed well, the administrator and the board must trust each other. If confidence is lacking, and if it cannot be developed, it is time for the school to get a new administrator. If a school has a succession of new administrators, it is time for the school to have new board members.

The nature of the board-administrator relationship is spiritual because the Christian school is a spiritual institution. When there is harmony, the Holy Spirit is not grieved, and He guides the board and the administrator in their respective responsibilities. When the board and administrator do not get along, the Spirit is grieved, and both are greatly hindered in the fulfillment of their roles by actions, behavior, and decisions that are carnal, not spiritual.

The board-administrator relationship is challenging in part because the board is the authority but the administrator is the trained educational leader. The board has the power, and the administrator has the knowledge. At times, the relationship resembles a couple learning how to ballroom dance when the woman knows how to waltz but the man needs to lead. Inevitably, some toes are stepped on as the teacher teaches the leader to lead.

More often, difficulties arise when inexperienced board members or inexperienced administrators have improper expectations of each other.

These expectations lead to misunderstandings and frustrations. Harmonious and effective board-administrator relations are built on the foundation of correct and mutually understood role expectations.

What the Board Should Expect of the Administrator

The administrator should meet each of the expectations listed below. Expectations and the extent to which they are met sometimes fluctuate significantly in a short time.

Spiritual Leadership

The Christian school requires that the administrator be the spiritual leader as well as the educational leader. This role cannot be delegated. Like board members, the administrator should meet the criteria for leadership in God's work, as set forth in 1 Timothy 3. No board member can set the spiritual tone of the school. It is the job of the administrator, who leads the faculty and students every school day. And the administrator must lead by example, not as a lord over God's heritage.

Respect

The administrator is the chief executive officer of the school, but he works under the board. The administrator must realize that this order is God's chain of command within the school. Much of God's guidance to the administrator comes through the decisions or directives of the board. The administrator must accept these decisions, even when he does not agree with them, without pouting or causing dissension. This submission means trusting that God is in ultimate control of the board and its decisions. The only limitation to this authority is when the board makes decisions that are contrary to Scripture.

Acceptance of Reproof

No administrator does the job perfectly. When the administrator makes mistakes, he must be reproved. God says that "the corrections of discipline are the way to life" (Proverbs 6:23). An administrator who refuses reproof is in error.

However, the board must be careful to reprove an administrator in a constructive manner. Usually, a gentle word spoken in private is the appropriate method. The administrator needs a soft heart, not a stiff neck, when these personal or professional issues occur. He must realize that the board's objective is to help him, even though it may hurt at first. The board must be gentle. It is not easy for a conscientious leader to be chastened by board members whose dedication to the school may be less than his since he is giving his life to it, with all the attendant sacrifices for him and his family.

Direct Dealings

One confidence builder for the board members is the assurance that the administrator always deals directly with them. Stirring up pressures against the board, politicking with parents or individual members outside board meetings, and working through devious channels have no place in Christian school administration. All dealings must be open, straightforward, and direct. The administrator should never circumvent the board.

Security on Sensitive Matters

To run the school, the board and administrator must occasionally discuss problems involving parents, students, and teachers. The administrator should be extremely discreet about disclosing board discussions or decisions with anyone who does not need to know. The board entrusts the administrator with much confidential information. Even a spouse should not know some things lest they upset the spouse or cause him or her to be uneasy when around the people involved. Likewise, the board should have a clearly understood policy that its deliberations on personal matters are not to be discussed with anyone who is not on the board, including spouses. To do otherwise is the sin of gossip. Unspoken prayer requests for problems are wise when praying in a group. God knows the situation, and it is frequently better to leave names with Him so as not to give rise to rumors. Private prayer might be better in these situations. Simply stated, security leaks hurt.

Philosophical Leadership

The Christian school was founded because God exists, has revealed His truth, and cannot be ignored in education. The administrator must have a mature view of God, His truth, and the world. She must nurture a clear understanding of the educational objectives that proceed from a Christian worldview. Through speaking and writing, she must articulate the purpose of the school consistently and effectively to the teachers, students, parents, board members, and various publics. The administrator must be growing, deepening, in her view of Christ-centered education.

Academic Leadership

No child should have to take an academic penalty in order to get a Christian education. Because the school is Christian, the administrator must take seriously her responsibility to lead toward academic quality. God is honored when the school is sound, not when it is second-rate in any way.

The administrator is self-motivated, for she is the educational leader of the school. She is trained as an academician and always growing in her profession. Just as a medical doctor keeps current in medicine, so the administrator keeps abreast of developments and trends in education. The difference between Christian and secular education is philosophical, and Christian education does not mean following outmoded approaches or using outdated materials. The administrator develops a school that is both contemporary and thoroughly Christian. That is her challenge, her ministry, and her delight. The board encourages the administrator's professional and spiritual growth.

The administrator leads the school in earning and maintaining its accreditation. Accreditation is laborious, and some schools balk at it; but accreditation is significant. Many Christian elementary and secondary schools have found that they can earn and maintain accreditation without compromising the school's spiritual standards. It is a straw argument to say that a school must make spiritual compromises to earn accreditation.

Straightforward Reports

It is the administrator's job to keep the board fully informed of the status of the school. She helps them see the school as it really is and feel its pulse. To do so, all the administrator's oral and written reports should be straightforward, without exaggeration or cover-up. Politicians are judged by their ability to spin news and events in a way that suits their purposes, but the Bible requires God's leaders to be honest in all things.

Wherever there are people, there are problems, and even well-administered schools face tough challenges. It is proper for the board to learn about the problems, or matters that could become problems, directly from the administrator rather than through the grapevine. The administrator does not report every picayune thing, but she is always completely level with the board.

Financial reporting to the board and to the school's different publics must be clear and accurate. The administrator must understand the school's finances well enough to inform the board about where the school is financially, how it got to that point, where it is going, and how it will get there.

Encouragement and Stimulation

The administrator is a positive person who can encourage and stimulate others to their best effort. He encourages the board, which can easily become burdened under the pressures of the work. Sometimes board members resign because everything seems negative, from the financial report right through the entire agenda. The administrator shows the board how God is working in the school. He urges board members to trust God in making wise decisions that are necessary for the school to progress.

The administrator must also encourage and stimulate the teachers, staff, students, and parents. Effective encouragement is genuine. If it is done artificially, it will hurt rather than help. The administrator is able to encourage others, while receiving very little encouragement or thanks himself. He is spiritually mature enough to get his encouragement from God, without requiring much human encouragement to sustain him when the going is hard. In the loneliness of leadership, he realizes that Christ is with him, indeed in him, and will never leave him alone. His purpose in his work is not to receive the adulation of people but to be approved by God. The administrator who seeks the approval of people will not have God's affirmation on his ministry.

Counsel to the Board Chair

The board chair, not the administrator, is responsible for reproving board members who are falling short in their responsibilities or erring in their roles. However, a wise chair will seek the private counsel of the administrator in evaluating the work of the board and its members. The board evaluates the administrator and should expect to be evaluated by him, not in any threatening sense, but toward the goal of improvement for the good of the school.

A periodic lunch shared by the board chair and the administrator goes a long way in strengthening their personal relationship, which is foundational to the school. This meeting is not secretive, but it gives the two of them a chance to talk heart-to-heart about the school, and that is wholesome.

Courage to Make Tough Decisions

Christian school administration is not an easy job; the administrator is under much stress. Not all difficulties are equal in intensity. The cause of the greatest stress is the necessity for making a difficult administrative decision, often involving people who are in the school or church. As hard as the decision may be, the administrator must not compromise the school's standards but must act courageously, without respect of persons, for partiality is sin. A strong administrator does not display indecision under pressure. He is strengthened when the board walks through difficult situations with him and supports courageous decisions; he is weakened when the board reverses his decisions and undercuts his authority.

Leadership in Discipline

The administrator is responsible for the level of discipline in the school. He must lead the teachers and students to the standard of discipline required to enable learning in the chapel, in the classroom, in the gym, and on the athletic field. He must maintain good discipline without resorting to coercion or setting a tense, fearful atmosphere that stifles initiative and creativity in the school. He must be firm, consistent, and fair. The ability to discipline by commanding respect in a natural way is essential to success as an administrator.

Good Judgment

It is surprising how many things come up in administering a Christian school for which the administrator's educational background does not provide ready answers. These opportunities require the administrator to exercise good judgment and to not be unpredictable, irrational, or given to overreaction or hasty decisions.

Good judgment is also needed for handling recurring problems. It is not always easy to apply the board's policies to the situations that come up constantly, even in a well-administered school. The administrator must have consistent good judgment, which requires an understanding of the Scriptures and the application of the Word to the problems of the school.

Recruitment and Retention of Personnel

No school is better than its faculty, and strong Christian schools are built on quality faculty and staff members. The administrative team carries the major responsibility for recruiting high-caliber personnel. It is wise to involve several persons in the interviewing process. The interview committee should arrive at a consensus before a new teacher is hired (Proverbs 15:22). However, with the counsel of the administrative team, the final decision must rest with the chief administrator.

The relationship between the faculty and staff and the administrator must be wholesome if quality personnel are to be retained. The administrator maintains a climate in which all faculty and staff members are developing fully while exercising their God-given talents. Good teachers and staff members often devote extended years of service to God in schools where the administrator encourages professional development and spiritual ministry.

Financial Management

The "other golden rule" states that he who controls the gold rules. The administrator is thoroughly involved in the financial management of the school. Budgeting is creative, for it begins with the educational program that the school will offer. The cost of that program becomes the expense side of the budget. Once the educational plan is established, the enrollment for the following year should be conservatively projected. Before the tuition rates can be set, a fee structure and a plan for any fund-raising should be developed, and the costs of all discounts should be projected. The budget will need to be revised and approved again when the actual enrollment and the projected tuition revenue for the new year are known.

Budget control is critical, for it is easy to overspend. The administrator has to monitor expenses effectively, taking into account the items that have been ordered and that are in the pipeline, as well as the bills already paid. Overlooking the pipeline can result in a misleading interpretation of the financial data. Fiscal responsibility by the administrator is vital, especially in years when there is a financial shortfall. Poor business management can hurt the school's testimony or lead to its demise.

What the Administrator Should Expect of the Board

Now consider the key relationship of board and administrator more completely by looking at what the administrator should expect of the board.

Daily Prayer Support

Board members can have a daily, unseen ministry to the administrator by supporting her in prayer. These prayers have a powerful effect, and the administrator needs them no matter how well educated or experienced she is.

Prayer keeps the administrator-board relationship harmonious, a fact of great value for the school. Daily dependence on God, expressed through prayer, honors Him and keeps Christ preeminent in the leadership of the school (Colossians 1:18). When dissension exists, the board and administrator have often not prayed for each other, usually over a period of time. Then when they do pray, they are likely to be asking that one or the other leave the school.

Appreciation of the Administrator

Christian school administration is not an easy ministry, and boards appreciate those who serve God in this way. Even though it is God who works in the administrator both "to will and to act according to his good purpose" (Philippians 2:13), God says that those who serve Him well should be appreciated (1 Timothy 5:17). An encouraging word now and then, a letter of appreciation, or acknowledgment of a good job costs the board nothing and lifts the administrator's spirits. A word spoken in due season to the administrator is like the proverbial apple of gold in a setting of silver (Proverbs 25:11). Of course, appreciation must be shown in a genuine way and without exaggeration. Sometimes board members see the administrator as an interchangeable part and forget that she is a person with emotional needs that include appreciation. Some thoughtful Christian schools have their parent organizations sponsor annual appreciation functions for all faculty and staff members. In contrast, one teacher taught in a Christian school for sixty years and was not even recognized or thanked at the commencement marking her retirement. God will not forget her.

Projection of the Administrator as the Head of the School

Although the administrator is under the authority of the board, it is she, not the chair of the board, who is the head of the school. The administrator is projected to the school parents and the public as the leader of the school.

The administrator has a prominent place in public meetings and in all school functions. Her name, and often her picture, should appear in the literature published by the school. The school is identified with the administrator, not just with its campus or its board. But the administrator must not lord it over those entrusted to her at the school, for she must always lead graciously and by example, as a shepherd (1 Peter 5:3). She is to be clearly identified, however, as the leader of the school.

Establishment of Basic Policies

A prime function of the board is to establish the basic policies within which the Christian school administrator is to manage the school. Establishing policies is an ongoing task of the board, for not all policies are set during the school's founding year. As time passes, certain policies outlive their effectiveness, and new policies replace them.

Board members must be committed to the process of establishing and administering policies before the problems occur and to supporting the fair application of policies regardless of who is involved. Board members who cannot commit to a policy position without knowing who is involved, or board members who reverse their policies for influential people, are respecters of persons and should resign from the board.

The board secretary should record all board policies in the policy manual, giving the date and the meeting at which the policy was adopted. The policy manual should be indexed by topic to keep the information organized. The copy-of-record policy manual is an official document, and the pages are printed and copied as needed for the board members. An even better method of maintaining the policy manual is to place it on a secure website, providing board members with an easily searchable record that is always current. Printed manuals tend to be consulted even after the policies have changed. When online manuals are changed, old policies disappear. The policy manual is also invaluable for orienting new board members.

Freedom to Administer the School

The administration of the school is the responsibility of the administrator, not the board, the board chair, or the board officers. Competent administrators will not work long under a board that meddles in the daily administration of the school. This approach causes divisions of authority and of responsibilities that create confusion among students, parents, and teachers. Board members should avoid spending too much time at the school, listening to gossip, or becoming its *de facto* complaint department. All problems and complaints need to be handled through the Matthew 18 principle, which requires adherence to the administrative chain of command.

Boards need to heighten their guard against becoming involved in administration, particularly when the school goes through a time without an administrator or with a rookie administrator. In times of emergency, the board may have to get involved with administration in order to keep the school functioning. During this time, the board must recognize that it is doing work that rightly belongs to the administrator. When the new administrator is hired, the board must draw back, allowing him or her to function. Veteran board members may have trouble turning over the responsibilities to a new administrator, but they must do so.

No Pressure for Favoritism

The school must be administered without partiality, or favoritism, which is sin (James 2:4). The board must exert absolutely no pressure on the administrator or teachers to give preferential treatment to some. The children of teachers, administrators, and board members are to be treated the same as all other children, without distinction. They must receive the same discipline, follow the same attendance policies, and live by the same rules as every other student. It is a serious disfavor to a student to treat her differently because her father or mother holds a place of leadership in the school. This principle is equally true for children whose parents contribute generously to the school. If favoritism is shown, children will learn that position or power makes right, that some people are permitted to do wrong. The other children will recognize the partiality and will not respect the administrator or the teachers.

Actually, the school has less latitude in dealing with the behavior of children of faculty members, board members, or donors. These children must receive consequences for their behavior that are by the book. If they receive mercy that might not be extended to another, the appearance of favoritism is unavoidable. The book of James says that teachers incur a stricter judgment (3:1), and unfortunately all too often in the school community, so do their children. An understanding of this dynamic should be part of the orientation process before a new member is installed.

It would be unusual if pressure for favoritism were applied in a regular board meeting. Such pressure is usually applied through a telephone call or is slipped into a conversation with the administrator. It often takes the form of a desire to not embarrass or offend certain parents for fear they will stop supporting the school with their money or endorsement. The threat of withholding financial support because of dissatisfaction is a shameful kind of pressure and must be avoided. Partiality undermines the authority of the board and administrator, and it grieves the Holy Spirit.

Courage to Make Tough Decisions

From time to time, important decisions will come to the board. Sometimes the board will not have unanimity about the decision, but after sufficient prayer and due deliberation, the board must make a good decision. If a board avoids making a necessary and difficult decision, the underlying problem does not go away. Avoided issues tend to grow into major and destructive problems. God will guide a board in knowing which decisions fit into this category.

The Will to Take Reasonable Steps of Faith

The growth of the school is closely related to faith in God. Faith is believing that what God says is true and then acting on it. But faith is not presumption. It is not faith to throw oneself off the temple roof and presume that God will offer protection. The administrator and the board members mix their faith to provide the leadership the school requires.

The leadership of a young school takes exciting steps of faith, including the purchase of property and the subsequent construction of buildings and athletic fields. Young institutions have a growth cycle like young people. It is vital that the school move ahead with prudent faith during the early years while the growth window is still open. Schools whose growth is stunted in the early years rarely mature.

Schools move ahead when the board analyzes costs yet steps out in responsible faith to purchase a campus and build facilities over the years as the school grows. There is a difference, however, between a step of faith and a leap of presumption. Faith responds to the provisions and promises of God, whereas presumption attempts to obligate God through some formula. Counting the cost includes having a prudent plan so that the school is not overburdened with debt.

It is not always easy for a board member to make decisions on the basis of faith, especially in matters of finance. Although a Christian, the typical board member works in the secular world where decisions are not made on the basis of faith in the living God. When he is about the business of the Christian school, this board member must shift gears, must change his outlook and his basis for making decisions. Failure to act by faith will impede the school. God is pleased and honored by faith in Him, and He blesses schools that exercise faith.

Proper Salaries for All Personnel

For some unknown reason, boards find it easier to trust God for money for land and buildings than for adequate salaries. Board members will make a decision to invest millions of dollars for a new building and then vote down a cost-of-living increase for the staff. Salary improvement requires faith, too.

Salaries are an issue of interest to God (1 Timothy 5:18) and are important to Christian school personnel. The board must treat salary issues carefully and fairly. Salary scales, along with benefits, must be improved and adhered to scrupulously. Each contract should be accompanied by a salary computation worksheet showing how the salary was determined and listing the cost to the school of all benefits including the school's portion of FICA. Employees may be surprised to learn that the cost of the benefits exceeds 25 percent of the amount of the salary. Every school should provide a major medical plan for their full-time staff.

Administrators may find it hard to speak to the board about their own salaries when they recommend improvements for the faculty and staff. Thus in some schools any raises for the administrator are erratic and are frequently out of line for the work performed. Most board members are not knowledgeable about the appropriate difference between a teacher's salary and an administrator's salary.

The amount of salary should be related to the number of contractual days, the administrator's educational background and experience, the size of the school, the grades taught at the school, and the responsibilities of the administrator. Typically, a middle school principal makes more than an elementary school principal makes. A senior high school principal makes more than a middle school principal. And a superintendent over the entire school makes more than a senior high school principal. Administrators of large schools earn more than what administrators of small schools earn. Administrators are paid more than teachers because of both their increased responsibility and the increase in their number of days worked. One fair means of determining administrative compensation is to calculate what the administrator would earn if hired as a teacher, multiply it by an index representing the additional responsibility, and then multiply the product again by an index representing the additional days in the contract year.

Annual Evaluation of the Administrator

The board should give the administrator an evaluation of performance at least once a year by January at the latest. The evaluation should be focused on the job description of the administrator and mutually approved goals for the institution. Incomplete or sporadic evaluations will not help the administrator or the school to mature.

Prayer

"Father, bless the board and the administrator by allowing us to work harmoniously together, even under intense pressure. May Satan not influence or break our strong relationship. May your Son be honored continuously through our work and our prayers together."

For Discussion

1. Why is the board-administrator relationship the key to successful leadership of the Christian school?

2. Why is it important to have the board and the administrator committed to confidentiality on sensitive issues? What problems arise when this commitment is violated?

3. Who is the spiritual leader of the Christian school, and what is the evidence that his or her leadership is effective?

4. Why is it necessary and beneficial to have straightforward communication between the administrator and the board? What factors can hinder communication?

5. Why is the courage to make tough decisions a prerequisite to effective leadership for the administrator and the board?

6. Who shares in the fund-raising responsibilities at your school? What are their various roles?

7. How is your administrator projected as the head of the Christian school?

8. Describe the importance of being a policy board. What is the process of developing and amending policies at your school?

9. Why is favoritism a sin? What forms can favoritism take in a Christian school?

10. How are salaries and benefits determined at your school? Who is responsible for overseeing the financial welfare of the faculty? How has the compensation package improved over the past five years?

11. How is your administrator evaluated? What is the process? What are the criteria? How could these be improved?

Going Deeper

1. Has your school board clearly identified and communicated its expectations to the administrator? Where is the documentation of these expectations? Is there a way to improve communication between the administrator and the board regarding these expectations?

2. What evidence is there in your school that the relationship between the board and the administrator is mutually respectful? What would be evidence of an even better relationship?

3. How have your board and your administrator shared in the spiritual, philosophical, and academic leadership of the school? How should they share in such leadership?

4. How can you better encourage your administrator in his or her multifaceted responsibility as the head of your school?

5. What helps you in, or hinders you from, recruiting and retaining quality faculty members? If you were truly committed to developing the best faculty possible, what decisions would you make over the next three years?

6. Does your salary and benefits package enable your teachers to serve God for a lifetime in Christian school education? Can they afford to buy a home and raise a family?

7. Are you compensating your administrator fairly for his or her additional responsibilities and extended days of ministry?

Other Activities

Have the board and the administrator work through each of the listed expectations, adding others as appropriate, and rank their relative importance to the goals of your school. A three-category scale of highest importance, average importance, and below average importance should be sufficient. Make sure that each respondent uses all of the ranking categories. Not every expectation can be of highest importance. Compare the opinions of importance for each expectation between the administrator and the board and discuss any significant differences.

7

RELATIONSHIP OF THE BOARD WITH FACULTY, STAFF, PARENTS, AND STUDENTS

Board members wear many hats in the school.

Board members, in addition to serving in a governance role, may often be parents of students, friends of department chairs, donors to the fine arts booster club, and business competitors of the contractor on the new building. Board members who serve well know the limitations on their authority. They know they only have authority at a duly called board meeting or such authority as the board chooses to formally assign to them. They never expect favored treatment by the school or its staff for themselves or their children. On the contrary, they are models to other parents and realize that if their children are involved in a disciplinary incident at the school, the children will receive the prescribed consequences because any leniency will be interpreted as favoritism. Good board members have many friends at the school and are significantly involved, but they must be able to take the board hat off when they leave the board meeting. The board must remember that the administrator alone manages the staff.

Relationship to the Faculty and Staff

In the Christian school, the board and the faculty and staff are not in an adversarial relationship, as is often the case with labor and management in industry. Faculty and staff members recognize that God has placed the board over them, and they act accordingly. The board must accept its responsibility for leadership while viewing its relationship with the faculty as one of leadership, cooperation, and teamwork directed toward the achievement of the school's objectives.

Friendliness Needed

Board members must reach out to the teachers in a kind, respectful way as genuine friends, not as bosses to employees. The faculty and staff members have a ministry for God at the school and are to be held in esteem by the board, even though the board is over them in the Lord.

Informal dinners and get-togethers foster friendliness by providing a relaxed social atmosphere for visiting. Times of prayer and sharing together in the Scriptures provide spiritual refreshment and the opportunity to be friendly on a deeper, more important level. Sometimes the entire board, faculty, and staff may be together. Other times a smaller number may gather, though care must be taken to avoid the development of cliques, for they are divisive.

Encouragement to the Faculty and Staff

Board members who give a word of commendation in due season follow a sound biblical principle. The word can be spoken in private or in public, depending on the commendation. A letter of commendation from the board can be a welcome reinforcement.

There are occasions when public honor is in order for the faculty or staff member, at which time the board chair may present a gift as a token of the board's appreciation. Some schools give service awards to their teachers on each five-year anniversary of their service. It is important for this program to honor faculty and other staff members alike. A janitor who has served for ten years should receive the same public recognition as that of a math teacher who has served for ten years. Some schools present these honors as part of the graduation exercises, while others present them at the annual school banquet. This practice, too, is in obedience to the biblical principle of giving honor to whom it is due.

Some schools also award board members on each five-year anniversary, on retirement from the board, or both. This practice is appropriate, and it should be done consistently, for board members deserve public recognition for their work on behalf of the school.

Sensitivity to Faculty and Staff Welfare

In Christian schools, there are no teacher unions to bargain with the board before contracts are accepted. The resulting silence does not mean, however, that the faculty and staff do not have serious financial needs. One good way for a board member to raise his sensitivity on financial issues is to choose a teacher or an administrator who has the same number of dependents he has, and check that person's salary. The board member knows what his own salary is and how well he is able to manage financially in the community. By comparing salaries, a board member can gain a better understanding of the teacher's situation.

It takes sustained attention and effort on the part of the board to raise salaries and benefits to a livable wage. The rule of thumb about what constitutes a livable wage is that a faculty member should be able to raise a family on the income provided. Eighty percent of a teacher's salary in a public school would be a suitable objective for many schools.

Many boards fail in this area because they do not work on these matters all year long. They simply set the salaries and benefits in the early spring of each year, and they do not include faculty welfare as part of their strategic plan. Rarely will such an approach provide a satisfactory schedule of salaries and benefits. The welfare of faculty and staff is important to their relationship with the board, for teachers interpret the board as insensitive to them and their families if it is unconcerned about their financial needs. Teachers and administrators rarely complain directly to the board about these matters, for doing so would be difficult. They simply resign quietly and take a position in another school.

No Meddling

Since boards hire and manage only one employee—the chief administrator—individual board members should not tell a school employee what to do directly. The board holds the administrator responsible for the management of the staff. Individual board members have authority only at board meetings, along with such authority between meetings as the board delegates expressly to them. Without such authority, a board member is just another person in the school community. In the world, rank has its privileges; but among God's people the one who would be first must be servant to all.

Relationship to the Parents

The parents are more than tuition-paying clients of the Christian school; they are God's agents entrusted with the responsibility of raising their children in the truth. The Christian school exists to help parents fulfill their God-given responsibilities.

Responsiveness and Authority

Parents are important partners with the school, and their input must be solicited. The board's thinking must also be shared with parents, apart from confidential matters. Practical avenues of communication between parents and the board must be established and maintained. In the school, the administrator is responsible for regular communication of the board's decisions. He or she is also responsible for communicating the combined thoughts of the parents to the board. Phone trees, email, and Internet technology open new means of communication. Paradoxically, the easier it has become to communicate, the more communication has become a challenge. Parents are inundated with such a quantity of information that they often do not read letters from school.

Responsiveness to parents never means that the board makes its decisions at every point according to the wishes of the parents. The board does not operate by the prevailing majority parental opinion but from the standpoint of its God-given authority for the task. The history of God's people shows that a majority has frequently been wrong, as the Old Testament illustrates often and well. A good board will never run roughshod over the parents, but over time it will make, for the good of the school, some difficult decisions that may be unpopular with some parents and perhaps most of them. From time to time, a school may formally solicit input from the parents through a questionnaire or the like, but care should be taken that parents do not think they are voting on an issue. Floating a questionnaire may raise parents' expectations and cause problems for a board.

Members of a board need to be discreet about listening to and talking with parents. The Bible's warning that people in authority must not talk too much applies here. Loose words spoken by a board member carry the weight of authority and have a way of becoming known to many people. A board member who is a whisperer, a gossip, or a talebearer damages the ministry of the school deeply. If that member does not change within a reasonable time after being reproved by the board chair, he or she should be removed from the board. The problems that such a member causes cannot be tolerated.

Matthew 18 and Handling Complaints

Every school should have a written grievance procedure that is clearly communicated to all its families. The procedure has prominence in the parent-student policy manual or handbook or even in the phone directory, the school publication that is used the most and misused the most. Questions and complaints arise inevitably, even in a well-run school. It is important to handle them courteously, politely, and promptly. Matthew 18 contains the most helpful principle: settle each complaint with the persons directly involved at the lowest level possible, even though it may take some time.

The steps for handling a parent complaint about a teacher or a teacher complaint about a parent follow the same biblical pattern:

- The parent meets privately with the teacher to seek a resolution in a spirit of reconciliation.
- If there is no resolution, the parent takes another neutral adult and meets with the teacher in the spirit of reconciliation.
- If there is no resolution, the parent meets with the teacher and the administrator to seek a resolution in a spirit of reconciliation.

- If there still is no resolution, in some schools, the problem may be presented to the entire school board, which then calls upon the parties involved as seems warranted, all in a spirit of reconciliation.

These steps must be publicized with parents and teachers. They must be reviewed periodically. Even after these precautions, board members must be alert to channel complaints that come directly to them according to the proper procedure. Only with constant supervision will the grievance policy function properly. There are always two sides to a story, and the wise board member will say very little, simply counseling a parent to take the complaint directly to the individual involved. A board member who does not agree with this process for handling complaints should resign from the board.

Parents must not be allowed to slander or intimidate teachers, and there will be times when redress must be given to the teacher. Over the years, there may even be times when students will be expelled from the school because of the deep negative attitude of their parents toward a teacher, other staff members, or board members.

On very rare occasions, a complaint such as abuse or immorality will be so serious and so confidential that it should be presented directly to the administrator or the chair of the board. Such complaints lie within the realm of matters that should be known to the fewest people possible, who can take whatever action is necessary if the complaint proves to be true.

Reporting the Status of the School

Parents are kept informed of the status of the school because they tend to be down on what they are not up on. Regular communication through known channels reduces rumors and gossip in the school community and benefits everyone, for Satan, the father of lies, uses rumors and gossip as part of his strategy to oppose the ministry of the school.

The administrator should give an oral report at the regularly scheduled meetings for parents. These reports are important and are prepared well, never ad-libbed. They must be clear, not wordy, and presented well. Although issues involving finances will probably be included, the reports must always acknowledge what God is doing in the school. Praise and credit are to be given to Him in all sincerity, "for it is God who works in [His people] both to will and to do for His good pleasure" (Philippians 2:13, NKJV).

The Internet offers schools communication initiated by the parents who access the information they want. Christian schools should determine what information would be the most helpful to make available to parents and then do so via the Internet.

An accurate annual report that highlights the successes of the year and reports the finances of the year and the goals for the upcoming year should be prepared each year after the annual audit report is received. The annual report is one of the publications with the widest circulation going to all current families and donors. Many schools include everyone on their widest database.

Informing About Capital Improvements

Parents must be especially informed about plans to purchase property and plans to construct new facilities. Good boards have vision; they are always thinking and planning several years ahead. Parents are typically not as visionary, and the board must be careful not to get too far ahead of them. The prayers, the financial support, and perhaps the vote of the parents will be needed to bring the board's vision to reality.

Balance is needed in this area, for a wise board will not say too much too soon about a capital improvement program. It can take considerable lead time to define a project and get it off the ground. People tend to think that once it is announced, a project will begin in the near future, but this is not always so. The board need not have everything finalized before going to the parents, but plans should be well under way. Specifically, both the plans for the building and the plans for raising the money should be just about complete. Both are prepared carefully, and they must rise together at the same pace so that both will be ready to go when approval is gained.

Relationship to the Students

The Christian school exists for the children and young people who are enrolled. The work of the board—the decisions of the board—must always be for the students' welfare and in their best interest. That focus gives clear direction for making right decisions about hiring and rehiring personnel. The school does not exist to provide a living for the teachers or the administrator.

Policies and Students

The board does not typically have much personal contact with students, but the policies it establishes may have a profound influence on them every day. When establishing policies, the board must think ahead to anticipate the effect on the students. At times, it is good to give new policies a trial period to see whether their implementation causes an unexpected and unfortunate side effect. After a trial period, the board can more easily change a policy that is not working. It hurts the stature of the board somewhat to set a policy firmly and then retract it because it does not work.

Personal Contact

Board members need to demonstrate support for the students by taking advantage of opportunities for personal contact throughout the school year. Board members should be alert to students and not spend all their time talking to one another or to other adults. Athletic events, concerts, plays, picnics, graduations, and special events offer wonderful opportunities for them to get to know more students. Prayer cards for students can also be signed at board meetings and sent to them.

A good way for board members to make contact is to speak in chapel. In a chapel service, the member can have personal contact with everyone. That contact is on the highest level, for sharing the things of Christ in chapel is a heart-to-heart experience. The administrator will be pleased to learn that a board member would like to be scheduled for chapel. However, he or she must use discretion since some board members are not gifted for that kind of assignment.

Letters of commendation from the board to the student body or to individual students are appreciated, and they build relationships by bringing the board a bit closer. An individual board member also has the freedom to communicate with a student when such a letter or phone call is in order. Such contacts are more impressive to students than most board members or administrators realize. Years afterward, the former student can often recall almost precisely what the board member said or wrote. Boards can easily commit to recognizing and commending one student from the lower school and one from the upper school in each regular meeting. Students could be nominated for this honor by a board member or by a faculty member and selected by the board. This program would also help to give a positive twist to board meetings, which too often focus on problems.

Personal contact does not mean that board members can show favoritism, especially to children of board members or the administrator or other teachers. In addition, it does not mean that students should feel free to complain to board members about teachers or the administrator. Board members should be able to discount any grumbling they hear. God's people have always shown a fairly strong tendency to grumble, even when they are in the center of His will.

Prayer

"Lord, help the board to exercise its proper authority while building and maintaining open, loving relationships with the faculty, staff, parents, and students. May it be said of the school, 'Behold how they love one another.' "

For Discussion

1. Why are relationships important to the Christian school board member?

2. What cautions should be observed in personal relationships within the school?

3. What are you doing to encourage and commend your faculty and staff members?

4. How should a board member address a concern about the effectiveness of a particular teacher?

5. How should your board solicit and respond to parent opinion?

6. What is your communications plan for keeping your school community informed? What are some indications of its effectiveness?

7. Do you have a written grievance procedure? Does everyone who may need to use it understand it?

8. How can you as a board improve your methods of commending your students?

Going Deeper

1. What stage should your financial and building design planning reach before you go public with your plans for your next building phase? How? Why?

2. How can you measure your students' spiritual development, which is the most important outcome of your ministry?

Other Activities

1. Study the faculty home ownership data and the teacher retention and turnover data for your school over the most recent five-year period. What evidence is there that the school is paying a living wage according to the rule of thumb presented in the chapter?

What improvements need to be made in the faculty compensation package?

2. Study the retirement saving and planning of various age groups within your current faculty members. According to current trends, what financial position will your faculty have reached when they retire? What improvements in the retirement plan are warranted to honor the teacher who serves God in your school for a lifetime?

8

INSTITUTIONAL MATURATION AND IDENTIFYING AND ADDRESSING CHALLENGES

All Christian schools, even good ones, have problems.

Some challenges are inherent in the maturation of the school. Others are interpersonal problems or ones caused by poor decisions in structuring the school.

The good schools establish procedures for identifying and solving their problems. The mediocre schools do not have such procedures and do not resolve their problems systematically. As a result, some of their problems grow until they become critical, and their solutions are traumatic.

Maturation of Christian Schools

The post–World War II Christian school movement in America is now old enough to have experience with schools going through different maturational cycles, some successful and some problematic. How a school will or should mature differs with church-related, parent-owned, and independent-board schools. School leadership and local demographics also greatly influence how a school matures. A school in an area that is declining in population will have a difficult time maturing even if it has big plans. There are common issues that arise in the life of a school.

When a school is very young—maybe just the dream of a small group of dedicated people—the people involved in the school may have to wear many hats. A new school that opens with a kindergarten and first grade will probably not be able to hire a full-time administrator. The board members will be involved in many of the administrative functions of the school such as hiring teachers and maybe even collecting tuition. As a school grows, the responsibilities will be increasingly transferred to more highly trained and specialized professionals. It is wise, from the earliest days of the school, to reference the standards of accreditation from the Association of Christian Schools and other associations for direction about these matters.

A school with 100 students will likely have a principal who does not teach more than half-time. When a high school is added, an additional administrator will likely be hired. The additional administrator will have gifts and abilities that complement the original administrator. As the school continues to grow, administrative as well as faculty positions become more specialized. When a secondary school is smaller, a science teacher may teach science to seventh graders and seniors. This teacher will have the calling of teaching the gifted student and the struggling student in the same classroom, teaching the squirrelly seventh-grade boy one period and the premed-focused chemistry student the next. Only a rare teacher is able to wow the middle schoolers and also push the high school Advanced Placement class and reach all of them. As a school grows and develops multiple sections, specialists are added to the faculty. Effective administrators are able to find the right matches in the hiring process and then maintain the optimal teacher placements as the teachers themselves grow professionally.

If the school is to mature, the board must mature. As the faculty and administration of the school mature, the board transfers responsibilities to the professionals. The board is able to attend to board work, and the administrators are empowered to run the school. Institutional maturation can be difficult on board members who like the nuts and bolts of school-ing or yearn for the closer relationships of a smaller school community.

In many Christian schools, institutional maturation has led to restruc-turing. Schools that were started as ministries of a local church have devel-oped independent boards. Some have separate campuses and facilities, and some continue to use the facilities of one or more churches. These boards realized that they were better able to minister to their communities and fulfill God's calling for their schools through a more independent struc-ture. In some communities, two or more struggling church-related schools have merged into one stronger, independent school by focusing on the essentials of biblical teaching and leaving instruction in denominational distinctives to the home and the church.

Interestingly, boards of more mature schools tend to meet less frequently, sometimes four to six times a year. As God blesses the school with a maturing administration, the board has less of a need to meet every month because issues that come up in the school have due discussion and process at the administrative level. Less frequent meetings can be beneficial by helping the board focus attention on big-picture, forward-thinking issues.

Structural Problems

No organizational design is people-proof. One administrator likes to say, "There are no problems at our Christian school ... until the faculty and the students come, that is. We all have sin and bring problems with us." Good planning and institutional structures can help alleviate potential problems, but even different institutional designs can be effective if the Spirit of God has a free reign in the hearts and lives of the Christians who lead.

Every school's organizational structure contains potential problems, some of which can be anticipated by studying the experiences of other schools. Knowing danger points in advance helps the board avoid many problems and recognize others as they begin to occur. Early diagnosis followed by firm action usually keeps problems minor. Left alone, problems rarely disappear. Instead, they intensify, forcing decisions that are more difficult.

Below is a list of some common structural problems. No attempt has been made to rank them in order of seriousness. Several of the following may be active at the same time within a school, in varying degrees of seriousness:

- One person holding different positions at different levels in the organization, for example, a teacher who is also an elder in a church-controlled school, a pastor or administrator who is also the chair of the board
- Close relations serving in different levels of the organization, for example, the pastor's wife serving as school secretary or a board member's relative serving as a teacher
- A husband-wife team, in which one is strong and one is weak, serving on the faculty
- A "wild center" of authority in school in which a group of people with strong friendships have undue influence on decision makers, for example, a regular golf foursome including two teachers and two board members
- An administrator who is not in control of the school finances either through lack of training or poor institutional design, for example, a treasurer or business manager who reports directly to the board and not to the administrator
- Failure of the board to acknowledge the administrator as the visible leader of the school
- An administrator who circumvents the authority of the board
- A pastor who directs or second-guesses the administrator of a church-sponsored or church-related school

- Domination of the board by the chair or by any other member
- An administrator who dominates a rubber-stamp board
- Failure to select board candidates for spiritual qualifications according to 1 Timothy 3 because of confusion over the difference between the spiritual gift of giving and the gift of leading
- Unwillingness to reprove board members who are not doing their jobs or who are not following the authority structure of the school

Maturational Problems

Some potential maturational problems are listed below:

- Having a "hands-on" board that fails to change its focus as a school matures so that administrators cannot lead
- Discerning the difference between faith and presumption as a school grows
- Burdening the school with debt that cannot easily be repaid
- Budgeting sufficient improvement in faculty and staff compensation while resources are needed for bricks and mortar
- Recruiting and retaining qualified, committed teachers and administrators
- Maintaining spiritual distinctives and focus during times of growth and especially times of declining enrollment
- Failing to purchase enough land when starting a campus
- Failing to develop a good master plan so buildings constructed first are in poor locations as the school grows
- Recruiting board members because of their standing in the community and not because of their spiritual maturity
- Failing to save sufficient money out of the annual operating budget each year to do the necessary major repairs to facilities

Interpersonal Problems

The following are some potential interpersonal problems:

- Parents are allowed to complain to board members without first going to the teacher involved, then to the administrator, and then to the board chair
- An administrator turns the faculty and staff against the board
- A member of the school stirs up dissention
- Nonsupportive parents do not value the spiritual distinctives of the school
- School leaders become respecters of key donors
- The school fails to adopt grievance procedures and provide training in this area

External Threats

Below are some potential external threats:

- Declines in the local economy
- Increased competition from improving public schools, charter schools, other Christian or private schools, and homeschooling
- Change in how parents perceive the safety issue on and near the campus
- Major demographic changes over time

The above lists are illustrative, not exhaustive. A good understanding of these pitfalls could keep a Christian school from some of the grievous problems that have deeply hurt some schools and closed others.

SWOT—Identifying and Prioritizing
Strengths, Weaknesses, Opportunities, and Threats

The first step to problem solving is problem finding, but there are dangers in focusing all the attention of the school just on problems. Instead, the school is better served by focusing attention on its internal strengths and weaknesses, its external opportunities, and its internal and external threats. Identifying and prioritizing these four categories helps an administrative team or the board in developing strategies to improve the school. SWOT analysis helps focus attention on enhancing strengths, addressing weaknesses, seizing opportunities, and protecting against threats.

In most schools, the administration is responsible for identifying and solving the majority of problems. In smaller schools that do not have an administrative team, the board joins with the administrator in identifying problems and developing strategies to address them. One method of identifying and prioritizing strengths, weaknesses, opportunities, and threats is presented below.

When this process is done with the administrative team, the board, the faculty, or a parent focus group, it has merit as long as the administrator supplies the leadership in the process. Doing this process with several different groups helps a school to better understand its challenges, just as triangulating GPS (Global Positioning System) signals enables a captain to identify his location at sea. The administrator is careful to fully inform the board as this process plays out. The board is involved at an appropriate level so it buys into any initiatives that result from the process.

Listing the SWOT Factors

First, the group brainstorms and lists, without discussing, as many different strengths, weaknesses, opportunities, and threats that currently face the school. The participants can identify the SWOT factors as a group or spend ten to fifteen minutes writing their own before sharing them. The goal of this session is to identify as many different SWOT factors as possible. As the group lists them, the moderator is careful that each item is indeed a different SWOT factor and not a rewording of a factor already listed.

The quality of this creative session is the key to the whole procedure. Members must feel free to participate in the right spirit, speaking frankly without being judgmental of others and without feeling threatened. This session should not be tense at all. Every participant wants God's best for the school. If the session is not conducted in a spirit of liberty, the real issues may not be spoken.

Usually the administrator directs this session and governs the spirit of it, but sometimes using another facilitator is beneficial. Extra prayer for wisdom should precede this brainstorming exercise, and participants should be notified in advance of what is planned so they can be prayerfully considering their lists.

Ranking the SWOT Factors

An appointed secretary then gives a list of the strengths, weaknesses, opportunities, and threats to each member. It is helpful for participants to have the list for several days to pray over them before ranking their importance. In a subsequent meeting, members are instructed to evaluate the list and mark what they consider the five most significant factors in each category, ranked in order of importance from first through fifth.

Members return the ballots to the secretary, who compiles a master list of the rankings. Importance can be determined for each item by assigning five points to the item ranked number one, four points to item number two, and so forth. A computer spreadsheet makes the computations instantaneous and shows the data for each item. With this method, the greatest strengths, weaknesses, opportunities, and threats become evident, and their rank order is the most important outcome of the procedure.

Determining Solutions and Choosing Strategies

The administrator bears the primary burden of identifying strategies. The focus is on enhancing strengths, addressing weaknesses, seizing opportunities, and protecting against threats.

This task is best done in conjunction with the administrative team or a small group of key advisers from the faculty and perhaps from the board. Sometimes an out-of-town retreat is the best setting to have extra time for creative thinking. Friday night through Saturday afternoon is a reasonable time period that does not interfere with family and church responsibilities on Sunday.

The problem-solving team should use the available time to work through strategies for each category, starting with the items ranked as most important and taking the time necessary to deal with each one thoroughly. The retreat will be successful even if it focuses only on the one or two most important factors in each category.

The first step is to define the SWOT factor clearly. This task is not always easy and may take more time than expected. It is a mistake to try to shortcut this step. Next, the group should consider possible responses. Members should think broadly and creatively at this point in the discussion. New responses should be considered along with old ones that have already been tried. As many alternatives as possible should be discussed. Finally, the best response should be determined, along with strategies for its implementation.

Sometimes it is wise to put a strategy into effect on a trial basis, for it may generate unforeseen results. It is easier to withdraw from a trial strategy than from an all-out commitment that does not work. After a reasonable length of time, the trial strategy should be reviewed for whatever revisions are warranted.

Resources for Outside Help
It is not good stewardship of time and resources for each Christian school to reinvent the wheel. There is competent help within the Christian school movement, and a local school should not be reluctant to seek it. The administrator should always lead in soliciting outside help and always be involved in the process.

Many opportunities for increased learning through workshops, institutes, and graduate schools are advertised regularly. Some resources are also listed in the appendix of this book. In addition to these opportunities, one of the best ways to seek good counsel is to pick up the phone and call a successful school. Administrators in areas that are blessed with more than one Christian school should be encouraged to meet together for lunch several times a year and sharpen each other. It is also beneficial for administrators to have an out-of-town mentor or confidant whom they can call to discuss the most sensitive issues.

Prayer

"Father, although it isn't easy, we give thanks for the problems of the school. Help the board and administration to admit the existence of problems. Help them to become good at identifying and solving problems by looking to you and by applying the principles of your Word."

For Discussion

1. Explain the concept of institutional maturation. Where is your school in that process?

2. Discuss the process of SWOT analysis. What previous experiences have you had with this approach?

3. Is this process, or a similar one, at work in your school? How is it being implemented?

Going Deeper

1. Which of the lists of potential problems are present in your school? Are any of these actual problems?

2. What Christian schools do you think of as examples of what your school should be? What makes them exemplary?

3. How much time and money does your school commit annually for the training and improvement of faculty, administration, and board members? Is this investment adequate? How could or should it be improved?

4. As you read the list of typical problem areas, were you comforted or distraught about your school's challenges? Why?

Other Activities

1. Commit the time necessary to do the SWOT process outlined in this chapter.

2. Identify and record past challenges and problems that the school addressed successfully and saw the hand of the Lord in. Count your blessings.

9

THE MARKS OF A QUALITY BOARD

Peter said in 2 Peter 1:12–13 that it was part of his ministry to remind believers of things they already knew, for this reminder would stir them up.

This chapter reviews many of the key themes addressed in this book by acknowledging the characteristics of a strong Christian school board. The following items are presented in that spirit.

Maturity and Growth of Each Member

The quality of the board equals the sum of the quality of its individual members. The foundations of quality are the board member's spiritual maturity and current growth in Christ, which are prerequisites for all service to God on the board. Board members may be alert and have strength in an area of expertise, but if they fall short in godly maturity and growth, they may do damage to the work of the board.

Members as a Microcosm

Relationships within the board are enhanced when members think of the board as a miniature of the universal body of Christ and realize that God is the head of the board. God has brought the members onto the board, has given them spiritual gifts by virtue of their new birth, and has given them responsibilities to fulfill for Him. Service should be viewed as the spiritual exercise of the body as each individual uses his or her abilities in the service of God and His Christian school.

Christ Promoted

The school's objective is to honor Christ in education. He is the one to be promoted and not the board. To apply a familiar Scripture, Christ must increase, but the board must decrease. Occasionally boards get carried away with their talents and their success, and they give the feeling that they, rather than Christ, have done wonderful things. Any inclinations to promote the board should be recognized and resisted, following the example of John the Baptist.

High Standards of Qualification

It is better to have a smaller board whose members are well qualified than a larger board whose membership includes some poorly qualified persons. Members who are poorly qualified dilute, damage, or even destroy the board. Nominating committees are extremely important, for if they bring only qualified candidates to the voters, it does not matter who is elected. A nominating committee that brings poorly qualified nominees before the voters does the Christian school a disservice. Board members who become disqualified after election must resign, or they must be removed.

Informed on Christian School Philosophy and Objectives

The Christian school is based on a biblical philosophy of life. Its objectives are biblical, not humanistic. The school exists because of its philosophy and objectives, which board members must comprehend to make wise decisions that will enable the school to achieve its purposes. They need a clear vision of the school's educational goals if they are to lead in attaining them. Achieving such a vision requires study, reading, seminars, and discussion to sharpen each board member's focus on what the local Christian school is about.

Ability to Determine God's Leading

As individuals and as a group, board members have to be experienced in knowing how to determine God's leading. They must make numerous decisions about issues on which they have no background or experience. Decisions must not be made automatically. Godly decision making starts with the desire to know God's will.

Unity in Christ

The Bible says that it is good for the Lord's people to dwell together in unity (Psalm 133:1). God gives unity, but His people are responsible for maintaining it. Board members need to show respect, care, and love for each other and for the administrator. Unity on the board is tangible. It can be sensed, felt, by everyone. Disunity is recognized and healed quickly. There is no place for a devil's advocate on the Christian school board.

Freedom of Expression

To deal with serious issues affecting the school, board members must be able to speak freely in their meetings. Two things are prerequisites for openness: a nonjudgmental attitude toward one another and a commitment to confidentiality. Board members should not feel that they must hold back from saying what they think about a matter to avoid judgment or the risk of having their ideas passed on. When members hold back, the board does not have the advantage of its own full counsel.

Exercise of Faith

The entire endeavor of the school is a walk of faith. The way of faith is always God's way, His method of showing that the school is not of man but of God. When His will in a matter is discerned, the board must exercise faith and obey it. Faith is believing that what God says is true and then acting on it. Schools grow through several stages, and there are numerous times, some of them critical, when the board must exercise faith if the school is to be all that God intends it to be. The board should never take the position that God is strong enough to get His people out of Egypt but not strong enough to get them into the Promised Land. That attitude is sin.

Prayer and Praise

Some Christian school boards are cheerful and happy in their work. Others are heavyhearted and sometimes depressed. The difference is not in the problems facing the school but in the heart attitude of the board members. The board ought to be characterized by praise and prayer, depending on God for everything and thanking God for all He is doing (1 Thessalonians 5:18).

Willingness to Work

Schools make rigorous demands on members of their boards. The duties are not ceremonial but require long hours of work. A major commitment is involved. Potential members should be asked frankly about their willingness to make heavy time commitments to the Christian school. Some board members purposely do not hold demanding church offices during the years they are serving on the school board because double duty is hard on the members and their families.

Strong Chair

The key to a strong board is the strong example of the chair. Even though members are volunteers, they need to be encouraged and then held to a high level of performance. Continuous exhortation and supervision by the chair is vital. The chair is a strong, visionary leader who is spiritually mature, godly, poised, and fair. In some schools, board chairs have a long tenure; in others, that tenure is deliberately limited in the bylaws. Either way, the chair is a strong leader.

Desire to Do Things Well

The board should hold itself to a high level, doing things right and doing them well. If the board is willing to live with a school that has inadequate personnel and facilities, that school will be mediocre. If the board prays only for grace to tolerate these inadequacies instead of praying for solutions, the school will neither prosper nor progress. The Christian school should be a first-class operation that is respected in the community. There are no shortcuts to developing a quality school.

Establishment of Policies

A strong board understands the difference between establishing board policies and administering the school. The board is responsible for establishing policies, and the administrator is responsible for administering the school within the framework of those policies. Supervision is needed to ensure that the board stays out of the school's administration.

Effective Board Meetings

Both regular meetings and special meetings are important. All members attend, informing the secretary of their impending absence if an emergency arises. Prior to the meeting, each member receives, via mail or email, the agenda, the minutes of the last meeting, and the most recent financial statement. This material should be studied in advance so the board member will be prepared to address each issue. Meetings need to begin punctually. Matters should be handled with prayer and in a businesslike way. Any new policies that are enacted should be entered in a separate board policy book as well as in the minutes of the meeting. The administrator should attend all meetings, usually having a voice but not a vote.

Major Decisions

Certain decisions in the life of the school are major. Therefore, the board should be nearly unanimous in making them. Still, board members must vote honestly, according to what they feel is right, not under a feeling of pressure because a nearly unanimous vote is requested. The problem with requesting a unanimous vote is that board members may feel that if they dissent they appear not to know God's will, and so they go along with the others even though they are not persuaded in their hearts.

No Partiality

Favoritism, or partiality, damages a school. Respect of persons will be detected quickly, and its outcome is always bad. Board members should never ask for special treatment for themselves or their friends. They should never exert even the least pressure on the administrator to be partial in a situation. According to James 2, respect of persons is sin.

Good Judgment

Good judgment is the ability to make correct decisions. In the school it means to understand the biblical teachings that apply and then to make the decision in accordance with them. To express it another way, good judgment from the world's viewpoint is often not the same as good judgment from God's viewpoint. A board that makes major errors frequently cannot merit the confidence of the school family.

Relationships Within the School

The board must establish and maintain quality relationships with the administrator, teachers, parents, and students. Relationships with people outside the school must also be good. A strong board does not allow poor relationships to persist but is sensitive in dealing with people and situations.

Problems Among People

In Matthew 18, Jesus speaks of problems with people and ways to handle them. To apply this teaching to the school, the people directly involved should resolve any problems at the lowest level. If they are unable to reach a reconciliation, the administrator, and ultimately the school board, may become involved. None of these steps should be circumvented. The whole procedure is to be followed with a gentle spirit. Everyone should do what is right and should have a desire for the healing that accompanies reconciliation.

Faculty and Staff Welfare

The welfare of the faculty and staff demands effort throughout the year, not just at salary time. The board should raise salaries to reasonable levels and should offer benefits that are comprehensive and always improving. Christian school personnel should view their work as a ministry and rarely complain about their salaries as do their counterparts in secular education. The fact that Christian school personnel do not strike does not mean that they are without financial needs. Their passivity in the area of finance puts responsibility on the board to become aware of their needs, paying them according to the professional services they render. Workers are worthy of their hire.

Encouragement to the Personnel

The faculty and staff are Christians who are serving God at the school, but they are also real people who need encouragement. Highly important to their morale is their attitude toward the school board. An encouraging, appreciative board follows the biblical admonition to bolster one another in the Lord.

Positive Leadership

It is important for the board to give positive leadership. The work does not progress if the leadership conveys an attitude of confusion, disappointment, or despair. Negativity from the board hinders the entire ministry. It is hard for the administrator, teachers, and parents to rise above the leadership of the board. A quality board faces and resolves negative situations while remaining positive in its approach and attitude.

Competent Administrator

Some say that the most important job of the board is to hire the right administrator. It would be hard to overemphasize that need. Once the person is hired, it is equally important to retain that leader and invest in his or her further professional growth. Strong schools have stable administrators who give their lives to the ministry a day at a time.

Variety Among the Members

Boards benefit from members who have a wider perspective on the school when they represent a variety of occupations, educational backgrounds, and areas of expertise. It is a blessing to observe and reflect on the ways God has been preparing people years before their election or appointment to serve Him on the Christian school board.

Careful Organization

Good organization helps to get all the work done efficiently. Organizational charts are needed. Job descriptions should be written carefully. Charters and bylaws should be in good legal order. All these should be reviewed periodically and revised as warranted. They are not constantly in flux, but they are subjected to review as years pass and the school grows. A policy that was good in prior years may not be best now. Doctrine is not subject to change, but policies, procedures, and plans are.

Changes in Board Positions

It is healthy to have some change in board leadership positions. When the same persons hold the same board offices or chair the same board committees for many consecutive years, they tend to become mechanical or stagnant. Changes in assignment are stimulating and encouraging to the board. Too much change annually can be chaotic, for board members require some time to become oriented to their assignments before they will perform at their best. A good balance of continuity and change is needed.

Board Turnover Not Excessive

It takes time for board members to become seasoned workers. If there is excessive turnover because of dropouts or because members are allowed to serve only short terms, a veteran board cannot be developed. The result is a board that is always young, with a limited ability to see problems in perspective and with limited time to resolve the problems. Quality boards encourage veteran members while bringing in new members as well.

In-Service Training

Members of quality boards are students of Christian school education. They grow in their understanding of their ministry through planned in-service activities, including the following: (1) attending conferences and seminars for Christian school board members, (2) attending workshops led by educational consultants invited to meet with the local board, (3) listening to or watching tapes made specifically for school boards, (4) visiting strong Christian schools to talk with board members and administrators, and (5) reading books and magazines concerning the ministry of the Christian school board.

Strong Board-Administrator Relationship

The board-administrator relationship is the key relationship in the school, for its quality controls the quality of the school. Neither the board nor the administrator should allow anything less than an excellent relationship to occur. That relationship is preserved, nurtured, and encouraged to grow. If it cannot become what it should after much prayer and counsel, the administrator should leave the school, or board members who cannot get along with the administrator should resign. No stalemate and no adversarial positions can be tolerated.

Sound Admissions Policies

Two things are controlled for a Christian school to reach its objectives: the personnel and the students. Although its leaders are Christian and trust God, the school is probably not equipped to handle the educational needs of all children. The school must develop admissions policies that are in harmony with what it is able and called to do. It is honest to admit that the school is unable to meet the needs of all students instead of pretending that prayer and Christian teachers can accomplish everything even though the teachers are untrained to educate children with special needs. The solution is to help the teachers get the training and to provide the facilities needed to educate children with a broader range of needs, a trend that has increased significantly throughout the country.

Obedience to Governmental Regulations

All relationships with state and federal governments should be clear and open. Particular care is taken with IRS matters and other matters involving money. Care is also needed in all dealings with the state department of education. There is wide variation among states as to how they work with their religious schools.

Financial Stewardship

The following are indications of quality in financial matters: (1) the board achieves and maintains financial stability; (2) budgeting is done accurately and soundly; (3) the budget is carefully controlled; (4) reports are clear, understood by all members, and always submitted on time; (5) the system for purchasing and payment is businesslike; (6) the school negotiates well to get the best prices; (7) the financial books are audited annually by an outside certified accountant; (8) the board does not overextend the school financially; and (9) the board is good at negotiating contracts for building projects.

Strategic Planning

Good Christian schools do not simply happen. They are the result of wise and forward-looking planning. Schools with adjacent land that is still available would be extremely wise to purchase it now or at least get the first option on it for future expansion. Then if the school grows, it will have space. If it does not grow, the land can be sold. Many schools deeply regret that they did not purchase adjoining land when they could have. Their vision was too small, and their strategic plans were inadequate.

Public Relations

The presentation of the school to the public takes planning. Actually the school has to be presented to several publics, including churches, the community, parents, students, pastors, alumni, and the parents of alumni. Various items may be shared with all the school's publics, while others will be presented carefully to one or two of them. In all public relations, the objective is to honor Christ. If He is honored, He will take care of the school.

Problem Solving

A strong school admits that it has problems, and it develops a procedure for identifying and solving them on a regular basis. Problems should be resolved at the lowest level possible. Since the solution may produce unexpected side effects, it is prudent to adopt solutions on a trial basis and revise them as necessary before making them final. Quality schools devote extra time during the year to problem solving.

A board retreat or an administrative retreat is good for this purpose. By their planning and forward thinking, good boards avoid some potential problems or conflicts.

Accreditation

Accreditation is meaningful in the educational world. A quality school should strive to attain accreditation if in the process the spiritual integrity of the school can be maintained. If any compromise is required, accreditation becomes undesirable. The administrator and the faculty, with the support of the board, do the greatest amount of work for accreditation. To maintain accreditation, a school must go through a renewal process every five to ten years.

Marginal Decisions Avoided

Over a period of years, a Christian school becomes mediocre if the board frequently has given the benefit of the doubt in marginal decisions. For example, if marginal administrators are retained, if marginal teachers are rehired, or if marginal students are admitted or readmitted, the school will not have the quality it should have. The school exists for the students, and the board must always seek the best for them and not be satisfied with the merely adequate. Over time, the accumulation of soft decisions has a weakening effect on the school.

The Sense of Serving God

The members of a quality Christian school board have a strong sense that they are serving God. They regard board membership as an honor, not for any prestige it offers but for the opportunity to serve. Members should be humble, for they realize that all genuine progress in the school comes from God. They realize that one of them plants and another waters, but it is God alone who gives the increase. At the same time, they understand that their work for the·Lord will be rewarded at the judgment seat of Christ.

Prayer

"Dear Father in heaven, work all that is well pleasing in your sight in and through the Christian school board. We pray this through Jesus Christ our Lord, to whom be all the honor and glory forever. Amen."

For Discussion

1. Do you agree in general with the list of marks of a quality board? Are there any you would add?

2. Which marks do you think are the most important indicators of board quality?

3. What common themes do you see among the marks of quality?

4. How do you think this list differs from one that would be developed for a secular private school board? Why is there a difference?

Going Deeper

1. For each mark of quality, list one indication of that mark in your school board.

2. For each mark of quality, offer one suggestion that would make that mark more prominent in your board.

APPENDIX

Resources available from Purposeful Design Publications

- *Christian School Board Leadership: A Framework for Effective Governance*
- *Christian School Strategic Planning*
- *Developing School Handbooks*

A complete list of leadership resources is available from the ACSI/ Purposeful Design Publications website at www.acsi.org/web2003/store.

Publications available from ACSI

- *Legal/Legislative Update*: Published three times per year and distributed to member schools as a benefit of membership.

- *Christian School Education*: A magazine for Christian school educators. Published four times per year and distributed to member schools as a benefit of membership. Contact cse@acsi.org for subscription information.

- *Christian Early Education*: A magazine for Christian early educators. Published four times per year and distributed to all member preschools as a benefit of membership. Contact cee@acsi.org for subscription information.

Professional development opportunities from ACSI

- **International Institute for Christian School Educators**: Held annually in July. Contact leadership@acsi.org for specific information.

- **Leadership Academy**: Held annually in July. Contact leadership@acsi.org for specific information.

- **One-Day Enablers**: One-day professional development seminars on a wide variety of leadership topics, under the direction of ACSI and held at numerous locations throughout the school year. Contact leadership@acsi.org for specific information.

Membership in professional organizations through ACSI

- **International Association of Christian School Administrators (IACSA)**

- **International Association of Christian School Board Members (IACSB)**

Contact leadership@acsi.org for additional information.